# SPIRITS OF THE CITY

# *Spirits of the City*

FLOYD McCLUNG

KINGSWAY PUBLICATIONS
EASTBOURNE

First published 1990



*Front cover photo: Zefa Picture Library*

**British Library Cataloguing in Publication Data**

McClung, Floyd
Spirits of the city.
1. Great Britain. Cities — Christian viewpoints
I. Title
261.83

ISBN 0–86065–776–0

Printed in Great Britain for
KINGSWAY PUBLICATIONS LTD
1 St Anne's Road, Eastbourne, E Sussex BN21 3UN
by Richard Clay Ltd, Bungay, Suffolk.
Typeset by Watermark, Hampermill Cottage, Watford

This book is dedicated to all my fellow YWAMers who have committed their lives to making the welfare of the city their welfare. May God grant you grace for the task.

# *Acknowledgements*

I am indebted to Ray Bakke and Harvie Conn for helping me think through the importance of the city from God's perspective.

I am also grateful to my wife, Sally, for her support and prayers during the writing of this book. The title of the book is hers, and for many years she has been teaching and equipping God's people about the importance of the spirits of the city.

I also appreciate my friend and co-worker, Pieter Bos, for challenging me to think through the theology of the city. Another fellow worker and companion of many years, Jim Mellis, has stimulated me many times to think through God's covenant relationship with the peoples of the earth.

Thanks also to Louise Beard, who spent many hours typing the manuscript.

And last but not least, my Amsterdam brothers and sisters who have patiently helped me work out in day-to-day life the lessons and principles that are shared in this book.

# *Contents*

# *A Tale of Many Cities ...*

It is the greatest mass migration in human history, and it will profoundly affect the life of every person on this planet. The explosion of large, multi-million-person cities is radically affecting economic and political policies. Some cities are industrial centres that attract hundreds of thousands of people hoping for employment. Others are cultural and education centres, luring the youth of a nation. Still others function as the seat of national and regional governments and therefore control the distribution of power and wealth in a nation.

There is no escaping the influence and power of the city. It has become the dominant social force in the world.

Cities are the mountain peaks of society—trends, ideologies, and fashions are born in the fermenting cauldron of city life—and then flow down and out to influence the populace.

What is the Christian response to the city? Are we, like some in the West, to see her as a threat to a secure and comfortable lifestyle? Are we to avoid the city as a stronghold of evil, and do all in our power to avoid the city lest we be endangered or contaminated by her inhabitants?

Surely a theological understanding of the city is needed, one that is firmly rooted in biblical truth, which will build a foundation on God's word for our responses. No other approach is sufficient for a truly committed Christian. Understanding God's sovereign purposes for the city is essential if believers are to have the inspiration and faith necessary to respond to today's urban challenges. Though inner-city populations are declining in Great Britain, the percentage of children between the ages of 5 and 10 living in London will increase 38 per cent by the year 2000!

The cities of this nation and the other countries in the Western world also highlight continued racial inequality and tension. The British unemployment rate for non-Whites is double that of Whites. In the 16–24 age group, 32 per cent of non-Whites are unemployed, compared with 17 per cent of Whites. The same trends are true for the United States.

Great Britain leads the rest of Europe in divorce. Alcohol-related emergencies cost the British public nearly £2,000 million a year. Teenagers spend £277 million a year on alcohol. According to a BBC report, research shows that the casualty rate of alcohol consumption exceeds twenty-fold all other drug-related casualties taken together.

Homelessness for the nation's youth is growing. According to *The Economist* on December 26, 1987, about 50,000 unemployed teenagers are homeless in London alone. Some 8,500 families live in council-found single rooms, and the number is growing. Many are Bangladeshi, Black or Irish. Those with rooms are luckier than the teenagers who sleep in cardboard boxes on London's embankment.

In 1985 the British government tightened its social security regulations. Its aim was to force teenagers to return home. Few have done so. Those under 26 who find somewhere to live must find a job or a place in a job-training scheme, or move on within eight weeks. If they do not, their benefits are cut by 70%.

The cities of Australia, Great Britain and the United States are magnets for the runaway, throw-away kids who cannot or will not live in homes where they are molested, beaten and rejected. Increasingly, the orphanages of Western nations are filled with kids whose parents, unlike those in the days of Charles Dickens, are alive but simply don't want them.

A crucial test of the moral character of a society is found in how it treats its outcasts. Modern Western societies will be judged all the harsher, not only because of how we treat our children, but because of the way we created their wounds. Never before have nations had so much wealth and so little compassion.

The Bible begins in a garden but ends in a city. God's redemptive purposes for every person include a community of believers that loves and accepts them, and shows the way to God's forgiveness. The heavenly city of God in the book of Revelation points to a way of life that must begin in the earthly city of man. To turn our back on the city is to turn away from God's eternal purposes of salvation and justice for his whole creation. To accept the challenge of the city is to embrace God's call to seek the *shalom* of the city. Blessed are the peacemakers....

# PART 1

## SPIRITUAL WARFARE IN THE CITY

CHAPTER 1

# *The Powers*

There is a personal evil being called Satan. He tempted Jesus, put betrayal into the heart of Judas, sought to deceive Peter, filled the heart of Ananias with lies, prowls around like a lion seeking to destroy believers, and is sometimes disguised as an angel of light (Matthew 4:1; 16:23; John 13:2, 1 Peter 5:8; Acts 5:3; 2 Corinthians 2:11).

All Bible-believing Christians acknowledge the reality of Satan. Spiritual warfare is a reality. It is the nature of that warfare that raises questions. Perhaps one of Satan's greatest tactics in attacking God's people is to intimidate us into silence on this subject. We are concerned about extremism. We have learned that if we leave well enough alone, we won't stir up problems. At least, we like to think that is what will happen.

If indeed there is a fallen spiritual being called Satan, and he heads a host of demons who are warring against the saints, then it is the greatest of all follies to ignore this warfare or treat it lightly.

This has not always been my attitude. I remember speaking to a group of university students in New Zealand in 1977. One of them asked me about my beliefs concerning the devil and spiritual warfare. I said, 'Satan loves sin, fear and attention, and I will not give him any of the three.' I then said abruptly, 'Next question, please,' thinking that by refusing to give time to even discuss the matter that I was treating the question in an appropriate manner.

Later that night, when I was alone and had time to reflect on the events of the day, I experienced a deep sense of sorrow. I did not understand what I had done wrong, but I felt that somehow I had grieved the Holy Spirit during the course of the day. I bowed in prayer and asked the Lord what was wrong. My answer to the student's question earlier in the day came to mind. A voice within me said, 'I am disappointed in your response. You have little knowledge of the demonic realm, and no authority over Satan as did my disciples many years ago. Your answer reflected your own fears.'

It hit me that I really knew nothing first hand about spiritual warfare, much less never having been used of the Lord to set a needy person free of demonic bondage. The words the Lord spoke to me that night pierced my soul. I had no spiritual authority in this area of my life. What was elementary in the discipleship training of the early followers of Jesus was a great void in my own life. I was responding in fear, a well-disguised fear dressed up in nice theological terms, but nevertheless it was still fear. It may have fooled some people, but not the Lord. I was afraid of the unknown. I was afraid of extremism.

The fact that there were people in need who could not be helped because of my spiritual impotence bothered me greatly. That night long ago in New

Zealand I read the words of Jesus from Matthew 10:1, 'And he called to him his twelve disciples and gave them authority over unclean spirits, to cast them out....' I asked him to teach me about spiritual warfare. I asked him for spiritual authority over unclean spirits. I prayed a simple prayer and asked the Lord Jesus to take away my fear, and to give me authority just as he had given it to his disciples many years ago.

That prayer put me in a frame of mind to learn. Nothing dramatic or emotional happened to me. But I started studying God's word to find out what it said about demons and spiritual powers. I wanted to know everything the Bible said about how Satan attacked people. In the process of studying the Scriptures, I discovered that not only did the devil have tactics that fall into patterns that can be recognised, but God has given Christians spiritual armour to defend themselves against the attacks of the enemy.

## Spiritual warfare in the city

What exactly does spiritual warfare have to do with cities? Any Christian who lives or works in a city, whether it be the suburbs or the inner city, without taking very seriously the warfare that exists there, is in for big problems. I am amazed that so many Christians are so ignorant of the spiritual battle that is being fought all around them.

In fact, I am astounded that so little is written or taught about this subject by evangelical Christians. I can find only two books addressing the topic of spiritual warfare as it relates to the church's role in the city, *The Meaning of the City* by Jacques Ellul and *Taking Our Cities for God* by John Dawson. This raises many questions: are we losing battles for cities because we are ignorant of the spiritual battles being fought? Have we unwittingly fallen prey to the devices of Satan? Are we bereft of the spiritual weapons at our disposal? Have whole ministries been defeated and churches divided because of Satan? Are the families of spiritual leaders and pastors being targeted by the enemy? I am convinced that the answer to these questions is yes. Over and over again, yes.

Further, when we observe the superficial nature of Western culture and its bent towards self-realisation, leisure, compulsive spending, apolitical passivity and moral permissiveness, one has to question the role of the demonic in the decline of Christian character in the West. Around the turn of the century a fundamental cultural transformation occurred in Western capitalist nations. Prior to this time, Western culture was oriented to the importance of work, savings, Christian morality, the nuclear family and even self-denial. Liberal Protestantism, the death of absolutes, the emergence of a therapeutic ethos among the educated in society, and national marketing forces, all coalesced to encourage this cultural transformation. While it is easy to oversimplify the suddenness or completeness of the changes that took place in society, the resulting emergence of a consumer culture is not. It is pervasive.

The erosion of Christian morality in every sphere of life was not just the result of the denial of biblical absolutes. I contend that spiritual powers are always at work when evil is present. Satan is called the prince of the power of the air. When men are disobedient, follow the passions of the flesh, and are by nature filled with wrath, their state is associated with Satan's influence (Ephesians 2:2). There is a difference between the temporal, or the seen, and the spiritual and unseen.

This is illustrated in the Greek tragedies. While the mortals act on one level of the stage, the gods acted on another. The audience saw a split-level stage with two simultaneous plays being acted out, totally interrelated but visually distinct. Likewise, the spiritual realm is unseen but real, intertwined with the lives of ordinary men and women.

When men are slaves to their passions, they are described in the Bible as 'foolish, disobedient, led astray...' (Titus 3:3). The Bible attributes this state of fallenness and depravity to having their minds blinded by 'the god of this world' (2 Corinthians 4:4).

Culture and fallen man are directly influenced by spiritual forces. This has a great effect on Christians. Leaders fall into immorality, wives become depressed, financial problems develop and good people turn against each other. Whole churches are being defeated and divided because of our ignorance and fear concerning spiritual warfare.

We know there are many challenges facing those who live in the city, and we will look at some of these in later chapters, but first we need to acknowledge that there is another dynamic at work besides the natural pressures and temptations that result from living in a fallen world. Why are there so many problems for Christians in the city? Are the problems people face more than just the need to adjust to the fast-paced life of the city? I suggest that these problems are not just the inevitable result of living in a busy city, but are also part of Satan's effort to defeat God's people.

We must also consider the social problems of the city in the context of spiritual warfare. There are large-scale problems of poverty, unemployment, prostitution, loneliness, chemical dependency, gang violence, abandoned and abused children, homelessness and AIDS in the urban world. How do all these relate to spiritual powers at work in the city? Is Satan seeking to destroy whole people-groups within nations and cities? Does he exploit the weaknesses of people, using their sins and the sins committed against them as a platform from which to bring them under bondage?

We recognise that man's greatest problem is sin. But if we ignore or downplay Satan's role in attacking and destroying people's lives, we are missing what God's word teaches us. Adam and Eve were punished because they disobeyed God, but Satan played a strategic role in tempting them. In the same way he will tempt people today.

The Bible says that 'we are not contending against flesh and blood, but against principalities, against the powers, against the world rulers of this present darkness, against the spiritual host of wickedness in the heavenly places' (Ephesians 6:12). God's word is clear: demonic powers are at work in the world. Believers are engaged in spiritual warfare; while we in the West can easily envisage spiritism and the occult in non-Western nations, we have yet to take seriously spiritual warfare in the West.

Demonic powers attack individuals, groups, institutions, structures and social mores in the city. Satan's tactics in harassing people are described throughout the Scriptures. He attacks in order to bring people into bondage to sin and the flesh. He tries to discourage them emotionally in order to defeat them spiritually. He will use any means at his disposal, and he will not ask permission first.

Satan can only do what the Lord allows (Job 1:6–12), but sin in our lives does give him a platform to harass and tempt us (Romans 1:18–27; Ephesians 2:1–3). He attacks people physically (2 Corinthians

12:7; Matthew 9:32–33; 12:22), morally (2 Corinthians 2:11), and in their thought life (Matthew 4:10; 16:22–23; Acts 5:3).

Satan seeks to lead the church into error, thus we are warned to 'test the spirits' (1 John 4:1–3). James also admonishes the church that there is an earthly wisdom that is 'devilish' (James 3:15). Paul envisages some teaching being introduced into the church at the instigation of evil spirits (1 Timothy 4:1).

Satan has established an advantage over many believers because of a widely prevailing incomprehension of the principles of biblical demonology, and because of a great ignorance of even an elementary knowledge of the power and reality of demonic deception.

## The powers

The apostle Paul repeatedly refers to spiritual powers which play a clear role in influencing events in the life of the church. The following passages in which Paul refers to the powers are cited in their New Testament sequence:

> For I am sure that neither death, nor life, nor angels, nor principalities, nor things present, nor things to come, nor powers, nor height, nor depth, nor anything else in all creation, will be able to separate us from the love of God in Christ Jesus our Lord (Romans 8:38–39).

> None of the rulers of this age understand this; for if they had, they would not have crucified the Lord of glory (1 Corinthians 2:8).

> Then comes the end, when he delivers the Kingdom to God the Father after destroying every rule and every authority and power. For he must reign until he has put all his enemies under his feet (1 Corinthians 15:24–25).

> ...which he accomplished in Christ when he raised him from the dead and made him sit at his right hand in the heavenly places, far above all rule and authority and power and dominion (Ephesians 1:20–21).
>
> ...in which you once walked following the course of this world, following the prince of the power of the air, the spirit that is now at work in the sons of disobedience (Ephesians 2:2).
>
> ...that through the Church the manifold wisdom of God might now be made known to the principalities and powers in the heavenly places (Ephesians 3:10).
>
> For we are not contending against flesh and blood, but against the principalities, against the powers, against the world rulers of this present darkness, against the spiritual hosts of wickedness in the heavenly places (Ephesians 6:12).
>
> ...for in him all things were created, in heaven and on earth, visible and invisible, whether thrones or dominions or principalities or authorities [powers]... (Colossians 1:16).
>
> ...he disarmed the principalities and powers and made a public example of them, triumphing over them in him (Colossians 2:15).

The use of the various terms Paul employs—principalities, powers, thrones, dominions, authorities—can be confusing. Hendrik Berkhof suggests that since a distinct meaning is never made clear by Paul for these different terms, it is not essential in order to understand Paul's message (*Christ and the Powers*, Harold Press, Page 15). However, it is important to note that, in the context, Paul makes abundantly clear the *general* meaning he has for them.

Our purpose is to focus on the word 'powers' as it relates to the subject of spiritual warfare with Satan for the city. There are several vital conclusions we draw by examining these passages:

(1) *The powers are created by Christ.* Paul does not hesitate to declare that all things were created 'through him and for him', even though they are not now fulfilling the purpose for which they were created.

(2) *They are personal spiritual beings.* Paul attributes the faculties and volition of reason to the powers (1 Corinthians 2:8). Further, he speaks of Christ disarming the powers and making a public example of them (Colossians 2:15). Something impersonal would not need to be disarmed and humiliated. Though Paul names the powers distinct from the angels in Romans 8:38, this does not preclude the possibility that the powers are fallen angels.

(3) *They influence events on earth.* Not only do they seek to lead humankind into all sorts of evil (Ephesians 2:2), but they also participated in the crucifixion of the Lord Jesus (1 Corinthians 2:8).

(4) *The function of the powers is to seek domination, primarily through religious means, over God's creation.* Paul stresses the relationship between the powers and their desire to dominate God's creation in Colossians 2:8,14,18,20. 'See to it that no one makes a prey of you ... have cancelled the bond which stood against us ... let no one disqualify you ... why do you live as if you still belonged to the world.'

The structures, religious traditions and philosophy referred to in this passage are not the powers, but the way the powers rule over men. In a similar passage, Paul says that while he was under the law, he was a slave to the elemental spirits of the universe (Galatians 4:1–3), reinforcing his teaching that the powers use religious means to dominate people.

(5) *If the powers cannot control men through religious means, they will exploit human passions and desires to achieve their purpose of domination and destruction.* Paul tells Titus that until the goodness and loving kindness of God our Saviour appeared, 'we were once foolish, disobedient, *led astray,* slaves to various passions and pleasures...' (Titus 3:3, italics mine).

Further, Paul names Satan to be the 'prince of the power of the air' and the one who was at work to lead us to live by the passions of our flesh (Ephesians 2:2–3).

(6) *The powers are evil.* Though Berkhof reaches another conclusion in his masterful treatise on the powers (page 29), we must disagree. What other conclusion can we reach about the powers since they crucified Christ, deceive men, exploit the passions of humanity and use religion to dominate millions of people? Though not the devil's *invention* (he is a created being and can create nothing), the powers are certainly vulnerable to the devil's *intention.*

(7) *The domination of the powers over God's creation is exposed and defeated at the cross.* Paul declares triumphantly that Christ 'disarmed the principalities and powers and made a public example of them, triumphing over them in him' (Colossians 2:15). Why then do the powers continue to harass believers? Defeated but not destroyed is

the answer—just as the Nazis were defeated on D-Day in World War 2 but still fought until V-Day many months later.

The exposure of the powers at the cross is central to their defeat, for their hold on people is based on a lie. Part of their hold over men is rooted in the lie that they are all-powerful and worthy of devotion. Through Christ's death and resurrection this lie is made public for all to see.

## The dethroning of the powers

The powers are defeated, but when the kingdom of God is proclaimed, they react. The preaching of the gospel exposes the powers; they viciously attack those who proclaim the good news, especially where their deceitful hold on men's minds is the greatest.

The powers are still present; the very act of declaring that Christ died and rose again is a declaration of war. Whenever Christ is proclaimed, a limit is set on the ability of the powers to deceive and dominate.

The presence of Christians is a reminder to the powers that they are defeated and a promise of their ultimate and final destruction. The presence of the church shakes Satan's kingdom; holy men and women are public witness to his lies. By her faith and life the church exposes Satan's powerlessness.

Because of this Satan retaliates. His weapons are fashioned from deceit, pride and fear. He will use every tactic possible to stop believers from exposing his work. Not ignorant of his devices, we lean on Jesus and his victory. We refuse to be impressed with Satan's ways, realising that when he is most frightened he makes the greatest effort to stop us. Nevertheless, we seek to discern the powers in order to withstand them and see them defeated as we lift up the conquering Christ.

## CHAPTER 2

# *Discerning the Spirits of the City*

It is essential that we recognise and respond to demonic powers peculiar to the city we live in. Certain kinds of demonic principalities are prevalent in certain places, depending on the sins that have given Satan a spiritual beachhead.

John the apostle mentions Satan's throne in Pergamum (Revelation 2:13). Whether John was referring to local religious practices, or he meant Satan had established his rule in that place, we do not know. What is important to learn from this passage is the localised nature of Satan's presence.

Demonic bondage is normally associated with individuals. But when one observes the moral disintegration of our society, the possibility of large-scale spiritual warfare against entire cities or nations seems possible. The Greek word that is used for principalities is *archas*, which is variously translated as beginnings, origins, rulers, authorities and rule. Bauer, Arndt and Gingrich say this term is used to refer to 'angelic and demonic powers, since they were thought of as having a political organisation' (*A Greek-English Lexicon of the New Testament*, p. 112). Concerning the term 'world rulers' used by Paul in Ephesians 6:12, they say that one use of the term refers to spirit beings who were thought of as having parts of the cosmos under their control.

That Paul uses the terms principalities, powers and world rulers in the context of 'this present darkness' (Ephesians 6:12) seems to point to his understanding of a hierarchy in the demonic realm that has been assigned to specific places and tasks. Paul uses the Greek word *exousias*, and it is interesting that this word is used elsewhere to refer to rulers and those to whom they have delegated their power, as well as functionaries of the spirit world (*A Greek-English Lexicon of the New Testament*, p. 278).

This is consistent with Daniel's situation when he referred to the 'prince of Persia' who opposed the angel of the Lord (Daniel 10:10–14). The angel said that the 'prince of the kingdom of Persia' had withstood him for days in his attempt to come to Daniel as the messenger of the Lord. The angel had been sent in response to Daniel's prayers. The phrase that catches our attention in this passage is 'prince of Persia'. Although we must not associate this phrase with the term 'principality' just because they sound the same, the concepts are related.

The angel coming to Daniel's aid was hindered by a spiritual being referred to as the prince of Persia. Evidently, a demonic power or principality was assigned by Satan to rule over his interest in Persia. This demonic being warred against the angel of the Lord because he recognised in Daniel an important adversary. If Daniel's prayers were answered, Satan's cause would have been dealt a great defeat, so the battle was on.

The Scriptures say very little about the nature and names of demon powers, so we must be cautious about naming spirits over places. What is important is recognising evil in the systems, institutions and lives of people in the city, and how that evil spirit manifests itself. Because of the association of evil and the demonic in Scripture, we may refer to this as the 'spirit of greed', or 'the spirit of violence' or whatever evil spiritual power seems to be manifesting itself in unusual dimensions in a city or nation.

If we have a view of sin that is limited to personal choices, we will miss an important truth: cities and nations take on a spiritual character and life of their own. This corporate spiritual character is potentially good or evil, dependent on the response of the people to God or Satan.

Further, it is vital to recognise that principalities and demonic powers seek to use wickedness in a city as a launching pad to attack Christians. It is essential that we do not enter the 'battle arena' without arming ourselves with the full armour of God. It is foolish to attempt God's work without a sufficient prayer base and an understanding of the spiritual weapons at our disposal.

Moreover God has raised up prophets in the church, some of them in the form of sociologists and theologians to 'discern the spirits' and alert the church to the presence of evil in political and economic institutions and society in general.

I am deeply troubled by the narrow view of spiritual warfare held by many charismatic Christians. God has given us prophets to warn the church, but their words are often not taken seriously because they do not prophesy with the customary charismatic trapping of a trembling voice during a prayer meeting. If ever the church needed to hear our prophets, it is now.

Discerning spiritual attacks and heeding warnings gives one insight on how to respond to difficult situations. My wife Sally and I have led a team in the red-light district of Amsterdam for several years. For the first few years every woman on our team who lived in the neighbourhood experienced some form of depression. After fasting and prayer, we became convinced that this was a spiritual attack to discourage our workers and close down our ministry of evangelism among the prostitutes. We believed we had discerned a particular enemy attack on our workers.

After many days of *prayer* spread over many months, this attack was broken. God gave us a new level of spiritual authority to withstand the attacks. However, there were very important steps that led up to the victory. Although the victory was the Lord's, we learned that he was using this situation to teach us principles of spiritual warfare.

God wanted us to *discern* that there was a spiritual attack that went beyond natural explanations for why people were suffering. He also wanted to teach us how to respond, corporately and individually. We began to *teach* our staff from God's word how to discern and react to the lies of the enemy and his attacks on their minds and emotions. My wife calls this 'developing practical weapons for spiritual warfare'. We must act in practical obedience to God's word, putting into practice specific scriptural principles that arm us with righteousness and spiritual protection in each situation we face.

## Discerning principalities and powers

Sin gives Satan a platform to attack people. Corporate sin in the life of a city also gives Satan a foothold over the city or institutions within it. After visiting scores of cities on every continent, I am convinced there are some principalities that are common to all cities, and some that are peculiar to particular ones. The spirit of greed at work in Monte Carlo and Las Vegas is unusual in its proportions, as is the spirit of sexual immorality in San Francisco and Amsterdam. Many people comment about the spirit of power at work in Washington DC, and how many good men and women have been blind to its work and thus fallen prey to its deceptive grip.

Violence, anger, loneliness and sensuality seem to be more than human problems in many cities. Satan uses sin to gain a foothold, and then he drives people to extremes, often beyond what they want themselves.

How do you discern when spiritual powers are at work? We must look for obsession with particular sins and an unusual 'drivenness' towards evil in an entire population. It is important to watch for monolithic deception in a city, particularly in regard to very basic areas of morality. When a whole population is being destroyed, it should put us on the alert, no matter what the natural causes. We must also be on the lookout for an 'antichrist' spirit, when Christians are despised in an almost irrational manner.

Satan often uses the problems of a city as an opportunity to introduce false solutions. He authors the problems, and then comes as an angel of light with a answer to the very problems that he started in the first place! For example, the dependence on technology in our society has produced an incredible amount of impersonality. The automobile seems to have driven people away from each other rather than enhancing the quality of their lives. People are 'busier' having fun, so busy, they have to work more and drive further to pay for all they are doing.

Has technology made our 'highly developed' Western nations more humane, more moral? On the contrary, the soul of the consumer machine is sick. We live increasingly isolated, lonely lives. We try to comfort ourselves with our machines and appliances, satiated with the best stereo sound, fed with food zapped in microwave ovens and overwhelmed with channels to watch on our cable-fed TVs, direct from satellites circling quietly above us.

Then the enemy of our souls comes along and says, 'Life can be much better. I have just the thing for you. You are living too fast. Slow down. Discover yourself. Look at the crystal rock, meditate and chant after me... Let's go out and have a good time tonight...' ad infinitum, ad nauseam.

There are four important characteristics helpful in discerning the work of principalities and powers on a broad scale in cities and nations: spiritual blindness and hardness towards the gospel; obsession with certain forms of evil throughout vast portions of the population; bondage to particular sins and behaviour that cannot be controlled by normal means used by societies to govern themselves; and compromise and defeat in the church (Romans 1:18–32).

Exercising the gift of discernment of spirits is crucial. We must know if we are battling demonic powers or dealing just with sin and its consequences in the culture. The two are not always the same. Further, if it is a battle against demonic powers, what kinds of powers are we battling against? It is important to know the exact kind of strategies Satan is using, and how they got rooted in the culture. There is normally a definitive relationship between demonic bondage in a city or nation, and the sins that have been committed on a large scale in the past. Sometimes we have to go back centuries to find the roots of some spiritual bondages.

Some years ago I was in a European nation for a time of extended ministry. I preached in several cities. After my meetings I was usually available to talk with people if they had questions. Over and over again I was amazed at how many people were struggling with deep, life-controlling fears. This pattern was so widespread that I began to ask ministers and friends if this was a common problem. They all agreed that it was.

I was puzzled about this, until a friend mentioned in passing that Christianity was introduced into this nation through a king in the eleventh century. He marched through the country with his army, putting to death all the citizens of the land who refused to become Christians. Christianity was born there in a national blood-bath.

I am convinced that events such as these profoundly impact a nation spiritually. Satan takes advantage of this kind of national trauma, and seeks to use it to establish spiritual strongholds. Principalities begin to work, and will not be driven out until they are recognised and the appropriate steps are taken to deliver the nation from the attack of demonic powers against the people.

# CHAPTER 3

## *Power Encounters*

The very existence of spiritual powers raises tough issues for us that must be addressed. What is to be our response to the presence of demonic powers?

We know we are given authority as believers to stand against spiritual powers of darkness because of the victory won for us on the cross by the Lord Jesus, but does that mean Christians should aggressively challenge the strongholds of Satan imbedded in institutions, economic and political systems, cultural norms and the lives of individual people?

This question implies a further question, and that is: who is the Lord of society? On the one hand we realise that society and culture is God's gift to us. He has created man as a social being, placed him on earth with stewardship over its resources, made us to interact with others and to live in human community, and established government to bring order and peace in nations. Because God is the creator of all things and the ruler of this universe, we may take for granted that it is his purpose that righteousness rule in the earth. The earth is the Lord's.

Although society is the Lord's, it is now also Satan's. It was the devil who offered Jesus the nations of this world when he tempted him in the desert. We recognise the reality of the kingdom of darkness and that man has fallen prey to Satan's evil devices. Often culture does not reflect the glory of God; it is fallen just as man is fallen.

We can take heart from Jesus' temptation in the wilderness. Though Satan promised Jesus everything, the Lord resisted his offer and overcame him. He went on to defeat him at the cross—Satan's shame was made public for all to see. The temptation in the wilderness is a drama now being played again. What Satan failed to accomplish in the heart of the Lord Jesus he now seeks to establish in the hearts of those who follow Jesus. We are engaged in a spiritual conflict, the outcome of which will determine who has the spiritual leadership in our world. The outcome of that first temptation is our assurance of the outcome of the second, if we fulfil the conditions put before us for victory over the enemy.

Just as victory was won in the wilderness through exercise of spiritual authority by the Lord Jesus, we must challenge the lies of Satan that he hurls at the world today. His strongholds are there, but they are vulnerable to those who resist them with truth and righteousness.

### The weapons of our warfare

Our primary weapons against Satan start on a personal level and extend to the corporate warfare of the church and its role in society. In the following pages we will discuss seven categories of spiritual weapons. Each category is related to the others and together they form a spiritual armour that allows the church not only to exist but to triumph over evil in society.

*(1) Inner reality with God*

Spiritual warfare can never be divorced from the foundational basics of trust in the Lord Jesus Christ for salvation, living a holy life, applying God's word and God's character to our business dealings and interpersonal relationships, fellowshipping with other believers, reading the Scriptures daily and being filled with the Holy Spirit. The spiritual armour for the believer that is described in Ephesians 6 speaks to the importance of the believer's relationship to the Lord and to others. Unless our minds are protected with the helmet of salvation, our hearts covered with the breastplate of righteousness, our innermost being girded with truth, our feet prepared to bring the gospel of peace to others, and unless we hold up the shield of faith with which we quench the accusations and attacks of the enemy, we are vulnerable.

There is no substitute for personal foundations of righteousness, servanthood, teachableness and hunger for God. If we do not cultivate these spiritual passions, carnal passions will dominate and control us. Unless we have inner reality with God, we will be overcome by other 'realities'. If individuals are vulnerable the whole church is vulnerable—a weak church will not be able to play the role destined for it by God in society.

Though inner spiritual reality and intimacy with God is the foundation for personal spiritual growth, this is not to be confused with modern individualism. Sin has always been built on the claim that we have a right to our own lives, along with the accompanying claim that we have a right to see things from our point of view. Though it sounds quite pious and acceptable to say that religion is a 'personal thing,' it is not true.

Modern individualism has so infiltrated the thinking of Western believers that we confuse the priesthood of the believer with a spirit of individualism that has isolated Christians in a kind of privatist Christianity. The consequence is selfishness in lifestyle and compromise of intellectual integrity. Our credibility and spiritual authority are thwarted in the public arena. As God's people we should know that individualism is a dangerous illusion. Christians are to stand against the world, but not alone. Together we are to discern evil in the culture around us, and then work out our response through corporate Bible study, prayer and discussion. And just as important, we are to practise what the Bible teaches in accountability to others in such a way that private professions of faith give powerful public witness.

Individual Christians who get caught in a spirit of privatist Christianity will face tremendous temptations to divorce faith from obedience, thus laying the axe to the root of Christian effectiveness in society. There are well-known examples of this approach to spirituality. An American TV evangelist once said, 'If I said it on the air, I believed it.' As if saying it made it true. The confusion and muddled thinking of this evangelist is obvious. This is an illustration of the breakdown between belief and behaviour, between 'faith' and truth. Just because a person says and believes something does not make it true in the biblical meaning of the word.

I fear that some Christians have not discerned the existential nature of the world around them, nor have they perceived the therapeutic ethos that has developed in our society. Inner spiritual reality is not to be confused with an experiential form of Christianity that makes subjective experiences more real to them than the objective reality of truth as revealed in the Bible. The wife of another TV evangelist was quoted as saying on television in response to a 'move of God', 'Fantastic, brother! Fantastic! Christianity is so fantastic—who cares whether or not it's true?'

*(2) Rooted in God's word and character*

The second spiritual weapon of our warfare is that individual believers and local congregations must be firmly rooted in the fixed realities of God's word and God's character. Os Guinness refers to an experience he had when he attended one of Washington DC's leading evangelical churches in his booklet *The Devil's Gauntlet* (IVP). The call to worship had as its confession on that particular Sunday morning, 'Father, forgive us for we have not lived up to our dreams'. Os called this the 'Hallmark card theology' and went on to say, 'American evangelicalism is awash in a sloppy, sentimental, superficial theology that wouldn't empower a clockwork mouse, let alone a disciple of Christ in the tough modern world'. This brand of Christianity has swept across Australia, New Zealand, Scandinavia and is beginning to influence believers in Great Britain.

While there is no argument with those who minister the love of God to a hurting world, the danger of responding to human need without sound, systematic proclamation of biblical truth is very real. To do so will lead to a sentimental kind of Christianity that is more concerned with healing people's emotional wounds than bringing them into right relationship with God. Fortunately, we do not have to choose between these two options.

There is a crucial moral change that has taken place in the Western world. It began with a shift from the Puritan commitment to salvation through self-denial, and has moved towards a therapeutic value system stressing self-realisation through a smorgasbord of self-help psychological and new-age systems. People are often more concerned with psychic and physical health than they are with their true spiritual condition.

Admittedly, people have always been preoccupied with their own emotional and physical well-being. But something different has happened in the last seventy-five years. In the last century, quest for health and well-being occurred within a larger religious and ethical framework. But by the beginning of this century, that framework had eroded. Now the quest for health is carried out in a world quick to embrace esoteric religious experiences but loath to embrace the death of Christ as their only source of salvation.

Acknowledging one's need for emotional healing, or desiring that from God, is not wrong. But when it is done within a larger framework of a society that seeks self-realisation, and the root of man's most basic problem is not challenged by the preaching of the cross and confrontation with the need to repent, then there is great danger that believers will be adrift in a subjective kind of Christianity that has little relationship to sound doctrine.

The need for emotional healing for the Christian is no different from the non-Christian's, but if this need is not addressed within the framework of biblical Christianity and addressed within the context of a complete biblical agenda of God's concern for our intellectual, physical, moral and social well-being, then we will not become biblical Christians but self-centred egotists who are merely using God to meet personal and private longings.

A consumer culture has emerged in the West that is built on marketing strategies which seek to convince people that to experience reality, sexual happiness and inner-personal well-being they must *consume*. There is a close relationship between the consumer culture and the therapeutic ethos of healing and emotional wholeness that has developed. Marketing strategists have sought systematically to undermine the Protestant values of work, savings and the family. Sometimes deliberately and sometimes unwittingly, advertisers and therapists have reinforced the spreading culture of consumption and self-realisation, tying the two together to appeal to needs for emotional well-being.

Where does that leave the church? If the gospel is peddled as one more way to be happy or rich, then we are more products of our culture than standing over and against it. When you cannot tell the difference in the lifestyles of Christians from non-Christians, the church is in serious trouble. And when prosperity doctrines reflect the cultural ethos of the world more than the biblical faith of our forefathers, the church must face the reality that it has been shaped by our culture.

What is the answer to this problem? I would suggest two simple requirements—authoritative, thoughtful proclamation of God's word; and systematic application of God's character to how we live as Christians. To do this in the present cultural milieu means nothing less than a power encounter with demonic forces.

The purpose for the proclamation of God's word is more than hearing our favourite denominational doctrine, or to hear the pastor's petty theological hobby horses. We are to get to know God through his word. In the process we are to learn about his character. We are to know his justice, we are to understand his mercy, we are to revel in his wisdom, we are to be conformed to his holiness and we are to stand in awe of his grace.

Jeremiah the prophet said many years ago, 'Let not the wise man glory in his wisdom, let not the mighty man glory in his might, let not the rich man glory in his riches; but let him who glories glory in this, that he understands and knows me, that I am the Lord who practise steadfast love, justice, and righteousness on the earth; for in these things I delight, says the Lord' (Jeremiah 9:23–24).

Such preaching means work. There is a story told of a young preacher who went to a more experienced pastor and asked for advice on how to prepare his first sermon. The pastor told him, 'Son, do not try to fill your mind with the learning of men or with fancy thoughts. Simply pray and ask the Lord to speak to you when you stand in the pulpit.' And the pastor said to the young man, 'When you do this I guarantee you when you enter the pulpit God will speak to you.' So taking the advice of his pastor the young man did not study or prepare ahead of time. In faith he believed that when he stood in the pulpit God would speak to him.

When the time came for the momentous Sunday

the young man stood without any notes or having done any preparation, proud of himself for not allowing his mind to be filled with 'human thoughts'. He stood quietly and prayed a simple prayer, 'Lord, I am your humble servant, and I have come now to preach your word. Please speak to me.' That Sunday morning the Lord spoke to the young man. This is what the Lord said: 'My son, you are not prepared.'

This story may be far more true than we care to acknowledge. How many pastors prepare their sermons a few hours before they rush to the pulpit? How many have not taken the time to seek God and study his word, coming to the pulpit assured of what God wants to say to his people? To quote Os Guinness,

> The problem is not just the heresy, though doubtless there is some of that. Nor is it just the degree of entertainment, and there is lots of that. Nor is it even the appalling gaps in the theology, for there is far too much of that. The real problem is that in what is said there is almost no sense of announcement from God; in what is shown, there is almost no sense of anointing by God (*The Devil's Gauntlet,* page 25).

The Sunday-morning pulpit is not a time for men to expound their own good ideas. It is a time for them to preach the eternal word of God and to do it with wisdom, understanding, authority and anointing, particularly being careful to discern the powers and how they are attacking God's people. They are to stand as ministers who have heard from God and bring the word of the Lord to the people. The written word is to be made alive by the flame of the Spirit burning in their hearts as they have spent hours alone with God, hearing what he would say to his people and saying it with conviction.

*(3) Worship*

Worship to the living God is a power encounter of the highest order. Subscribing to any object, or being, devotion that belongs to God is a sin; it is yielding to the temptations presented by the devil to Jesus in the wilderness. We are engaged in the same battle as Jesus. Satan seeks to lure us if he can, and manipulate us if he cannot, to redirect our worship and trust away from the living God.

Not only are we presented with opportunities to worship false gods, Satan also seeks to stifle our worship by undermining our faith in God. If our focus is dominated by the problems of the city, and we develop a negative outlook, it will affect our worship of God. While problems are not be ignored or denied, God and his goodness must be central to our Christian life.

God demonstrated to the people of Israel the significance of worship in spiritual warfare by defeating Judah's enemies through the singing of praise instead of military power (2 Chronicles 20:21–22).

John Dawson reminds us of this powerful truth in his book *Taking Our Cities for God* (Creation House, page 164):

> The New Testament Greek word for worship, *proskuneo,* means 'to kiss toward', implying emotional response toward God. Our heartfelt expressions of praise are rooted in the discipline of thanksgiving. To be grateful is consciously to acknowledge our debt to another, and this is an activity we are to choose: 'Always and for everything giving thanks in the name of our Lord Jesus Christ to God the Father.' (Ephesians 5:20)
>
> The opposite behavior—murmuring and complain-

> ing—is a sin that God will not tolerate. Such conduct poisons the atmosphere, robs others of their faith and produces death and defeat. When the children of Israel murmured against Moses and Aaron, 14,700 of them were smitten with a plague and died (see Numbers 16:49).

Dawson goes on to point out that while we hesitate to slander people openly and directly, we think it is acceptable to murmur against the city we live in because of its supposedly impersonal nature. But the issue that motivated Israel's complaint against Moses was also their environment. 'Moreover you have not brought us into a land flowing with milk and honey, nor given us inheritance of fields and vineyards' (Numbers 16:14).

I have heard countless Christians slander the city they live in, as if the reality of the problems excused their negative attitudes. Such criticalness is a breeding ground for unbelief. They focus on the problems and become more impressed with Satan's power than God's. Sin in a city *is* offensive to the spiritually sensitive person. It is grievous to see the pollution hovering in grey clouds over large cities. It is hurtful to one's spirit to see large numbers of young men and women being exploited by sex-mad pimps and purveyors of pornography. Anger seems the only appropriate response to the oppression and injustice highlighted in third-world urban slum areas and first-world inner cities. Dirt and destruction in cities is offensive.

But the key issue is how we should respond to all this. It exists. It is evil. It is repugnant to see. But should we respond with hardness of heart and criticalness?

What has this to do with worship in the city? Worship is more than what we do for an hour or two on Sundays. It is an attitude of life. It is a lifestyle. It is being focused on the goodness of God and the assurance of his desire to bless all people in spite of the corruption and arrogance of sinful humanity.

Without worship we will be overwhelmed by the needs of the city. We will develop cynicism and unbelief. Our service to God will be tainted by bitterness. Our existence will be motivated by escape. We will be dominated by the city instead of rising above its problems.

Worship releases understanding of God's heart for people. It creates a highway from God's heart to ours. We see the city, in spite of its problems, in the light of God's destiny for his people in that place. We begin to see with eyes of faith what God wants to do in and through his people.

Regular corporate worship magnifies what is in the hearts of individuals. If we come with a heart of thanksgiving that is fuelled by regular study of God's word, and focus on God's character, worship with the community of the believers feeds our souls.

The presence of worshipping Christians in a needy city is a powerful challenge to the powers of darkness. We are challenging the hold of Satan on people's lives. We are a reminder that he has been defeated. Our worship is a serious threat to the hold he has on people, a hold which is powered by the illusion that he is all-powerful.

*(4) Research and analysis*

Another spiritual set of weapons in contesting Satan's efforts to destroy the city, is to discern through research and tough-minded analysis the issues that challenge the influence of the gospel in the city. There is a deep rooted anti-intellectualism in the church that has caused us to be ineffective not only in reaching thinking non-Christians, but also in influencing the direction of our culture. When we do not encourage the exercise of the intellectual gifts that God has given to the church it means we are disobedient, anti-spiritual and unloving. Only through thinking in a tough-minded manner about the political, economic and social issues that face us in the city, can we hope to exercise the influence that God has intended for us as Christians to have. This is a matter of Christian faithfulness and integrity. We need a clearer grasp of the complex nature of the city, and God's purposes for it in its redeemed form (see Chapter 4).

Os Guinness gives us insight in a story he tells in his booklet, *The Devil's Gauntlet.* He relates a story told by Nikita Khrushchev about a time when there was a wave of petty theft in the Soviet Union. To curtail this the authorities put up guards around factories. At one factory in Leningrad, the guard knew the workers in the factory well. The first evening, out came Pyotr Petrovich with a wheelbarrow, and on the wheelbarrow a great bulky sack with a suspicious-looking object inside.

'All right, Petrovich,' said the guard, 'what have you got there in that sack?'

'Oh, just sawdust and shavings,' Petrovich replied.

'Come on,' the guard said, 'I wasn't born yesterday. Tip it out.' Petrovich obliged and poured out the contents of the sack. Out came nothing but sawdust and shavings. So he was allowed to put it all back again in the wheelbarrow and go home.

When the same thing happened every night of the week, the guard became frustrated. Finally, his curiosity overcame his frustration.

'Petrovich,' he said, 'I know you. Tell me what you are smuggling in those sacks, and I will let you go.'

'I'm not smuggling anything in the sacks,' said Petrovich. 'I'm smuggling wheelbarrows, my friend, wheelbarrows.'

The church has set up guards to check for secular humanism and the New Age, and the devil has smuggled modernism right past our noses and into the church. The church is surrounded by a monolithic culture that is saturated in non-biblical values. Yet we cannot see the wood for the trees. While trying to fight for theological purity and against new age conspiracies, we have become a compromised church that is more worldly than anything we could have imagined.

Sanctified minds need to examine the influence of culture *in its totality* on the church. Every part of life is impregnated by a culture totally at odds with godliness and Christian witness. Spiritual warfare at this point pulls down strongholds by hard thinking. We need prayer, yes, but we also need prophetic sociologists to point out the betrayal of the gospel in Western culture.

Worldliness attacks the church by luring us into compromise on the absolutes of our faith. But we are also tempted by Satan to participate in unethical fund raising, superficial fellowship, ungodly dependence on technology, manipulation by information systems and compromise by worldly educational philosophies and techniques. Unless we are thinking carefully about our lifestyle and how it effects our financial dealings, our relationships, the use of our time, our ambitions and dreams, and the rearing of our family, we will soon be swallowed up by a society that pulls us away from biblical Christianity in the most basic functions of life. If Christians are not aware how totally dependent they have become on systems of education, transportation and communication that by their very nature lead to worldliness in new forms, we will be overwhelmed by one of Satan's most subtle but devastating attacks on the church in the last 2,000 years.

We must not soothe our consciences by giving handouts to the poor and counselling the wounded. Nor can we afford to look at the increasing numbers of our church and feel smug. If we develop a narrow agenda of social and moral issues and pat ourselves on the back as if we have done enough, we delude ourselves. Our lack of awareness of the battles that are being fought in the universities and political think-tanks of our nation has catastrophic consequences.

We who live in the West must repent for turning the great ideals of liberty and prosperity into modern-day idols. Liberty has become a licence to live for ourselves, and prosperity is adored as the goal of life, rather than the result of honesty and hard work. We have been blinded by these idols so that we cannot see the multitude of evils that are taking place in the economic and social arenas around us.

*(5) Fervent intercession*

If we are to discern the battle fronts rightly, we must not only think in a tough-minded manner, but we must be linked with fervent intercessors who are listening carefully to what God has on his heart for our cities. A group of women that are associated with Christ Our Shepherd Church in

Washington DC were praying in 1984 for the city. During the time of prayer, one of the women felt that the Lord was putting it on her heart to intercede for the influence of astrology on Nancy Reagan. At that time it had not been made public that Mrs Reagan was seriously and systematically seeking the counsel and advice of an astrologer. When the news broke some time later, the prayer group felt it was in response to their prayers that God would expose what was 'hidden in darkness'.

Intercession is not an occupation for little old ladies who have nothing better to do with their time, but stands central to the church's mission in society. Even for those not clued into the battles being fought for the minds of men on the geopolitical levels, windows of insight are given through intercession that should be linked to those fighting on the intellectual front. Nehemiah joined those working on the walls of Jerusalem, telling them that if the enemy attacked in one place they should blow their trumpet to rally the help of others. This integration of intercession and intellectual pursuit of truth is vital. Either pursuit alone risks the danger of producing a warm-hearted but ill-informed zeal on the one hand, or a cold-hearted and aloof intellectualism on the other hand.

Those who take seriously the needs of the city must guard against a detached type of intercession that does not lead to identification with the needs of the people they are praying for. Identification with people makes our praying real. John Dawson says,

> Intercession is not an escape from reality. Our communication with God must be rooted in the truth—the eternal truth of His holy standards and the

> awful truth about our society as God sees it. The intercessor experiences the broken heart of God through the indwelling presence of the Holy Spirit. The intercessor also identifies with the sin of the people, because the intercessor has personally contributed to God's grief. (*Taking Our Cities for God,* page 184)

I not only have the privilege of living in a major inner-city, I travel constantly, speaking about our work. I love the thrill of declaring God's purposes for cities to audiences large and small. But being away from direct ministry involvement on the streets due to my speaking ministry, and being saddled with inescapable administrative responsibilities, has taken its toll. I have sometimes found myself speaking about experiences from further and further in the past, without up-to-date contact with people in my neighbourhood. Sometimes I am forced to accept this as part of the price of an international calling to challenge others to get involved.

What I cannot accept is cold-heartedness due to lack of identification and intercession. When my prayer life suffers from lack of discipline, everything else is affected. Sermon illustrations become just that: sermon illustrations.

But when I pray with passion, and when I identify with the sins of the people (Nehemiah 1), things begin to change. Not only do I speak with a greater authority, my life back in Amsterdam is deeply impacted. I get more involved with people spontaneously, and I partake in the spiritual heartthrob of the city. Prayer keeps me from being a spectator. Identification keeps me in tune on a heart level.

When we prepare a team to go to another city from Amsterdam for evangelism, we first do research into the historical, cultural and spiritual background of the city. When the team arrives in the city they walk the streets two-by-two, interceding until they sense that they have discerned the spiritual forces that are at work in the city. They then pray specifically for breakthroughs in these areas. This kind of intercession is not a substitute for residency or analysis of issues, but is central to all other forms of spiritual warfare and Christian service. It provides the heart-link to God's heart, and the integration point for the total effort of Christian mission. It is the 'nervous system' of the church's response to the powers, linking all our efforts in a concerted and co-ordinated response.

Prayer teams are desperately needed by those who are engaged in the public arena, and vice-versa. Satan uses people to obstruct the purposes of God, even well-meaning believers. Many a sincere politician or public servant has found his greatest opposition coming from other Christians. This should not surprise us, nor should we divorce this opposition from Satan's tactics. It was Peter who told Jesus he should not go to Jerusalem to die on the cross. Recognising the source of Peter's grand idea, Jesus looked at Peter and spoke to Satan: 'Get behind me, Satan!' It is through prayer—the exercising of the authority we have in Jesus' name—that we win spiritual battles.

We see this marriage of mind and spirit, prayer and research, in the life of Nehemiah. Nehemiah heard a report about the broken walls of Jerusalem while he was in exile in Babylon. He was so disturbed by the report that it moved him to days of fasting, prayer and weeping over the spiritual state of his people. When he finally received permission to return to Jerusalem to do something about this problem, before he announced any plans or launched any programmes he first of all surveyed the walls of the city very carefully. Nehemiah took time to examine the walls to make sure he understood their exact condition. What he saw when he looked them over confirmed what he had discerned through prayer.

There is a great need in Christian leadership for those who are both broken-hearted and tough-minded, people who are dove-gentle and yet serpent-wise. This kind of Christianity can be a great tool in the hands of God and a great weapon against the forces of darkness.

*(6) Church unity*

The unity of the church in the city is warfare against spiritual powers. The apostle Paul declares that we are seated with Christ in the heavenly places, *together* with all the saints (Ephesians 2:6). This verse speaks of the authority of those who are in Christ. It implies that this authority comes from being seated with Christ in his place of divine rule as a united church. We experience that authority if we are in Christ, with other believers. Notice how often Paul writes 'us' and 'our' in this passage: 'Even when we were dead through our trespasses, [he] made us alive together with Christ (by grace you have been saved), and raised us up with him, and made us sit with him in the heavenly places in Christ Jesus' (Ephesians 2:5–6).

The context is our victory over evil and the powers of darkness (Ephesians 2:2). Paul paints a picture for us of a church that is seated *together* with Christ in his place of authority ruling over the powers; but he makes it clear that our authority is directly related to our unity.

Lived out, this truth points the way to openness,

interdependence and accountability as a way of life. However, most believers are shocked at the thought of seeking advice about their family and business dealings, much less feeling a responsibility to include others in the important decisions they make. Has the Western church lost its spiritual authority because it has been compromised in this vital element of biblical church life? The influence of modern industrialisation may be so monolithic that we find those things that were natural and spontaneous in the early church extraneous to our way of living and thinking.

It seems from a casual reading of Scripture that the elders of New Testament churches were functioning in close relationship with one another. This 'connectedness' of church leaders is missing today. The church will not have the authority promised in Scripture until it is restored. The unity implied in Ephesians 2 is dynamic and powerful. It is not a passive unity, but an active unity, one that must be *pursued*.

Even when there is a difference in perspective or emphasis among Christians today, they are minor compared to the battles being fought by the whole church against the powers in the city. We must rise above our normal theological differences, allow one another freedom to 'be wrong' sometimes and find common ground to stand together in Christ against the spiritual powers dominating our cities—and our churches. We must do this because we know that 'God opposes the proud, but gives grace to the humble' (James 4:6–7).

Where biblical unity exists, we can lovingly disagree and still get on with the business of setting people free from sin and challenging the powers and their influence in public institutions and policy. (For a fuller discussion of the nature of biblical unity, see my book *Father Make Us One* [Kingsway].) This unity will express itself in a spirit of teachableness and servanthood. By maintaining a humble and teachable attitude, while holding to our personal theological convictions, we can fellowship with believers of various denominations. This paves the way to build the kind of unity in a city that is absolutely essential for overcoming spiritual powers.

The Moravians used to teach that fellowship among Christians was a sacrament of the church, a means of God giving grace to his people. City life has become so hectic, so filled with sensory overload, that it leaves people emotionally depleted. The temptation is to narrow our contacts with other believers to the level that is necessary for 'survival'. When this happens we may have more time for ourselves, but we are on dangerous spiritual ground.

By being cut off from meaningful relationships with other believers, Satan wins a victory and the first step has been taken to denigrate the church. City believers need fellowship with other Christians, and they will have to fight the busyness of the city to achieve it. We cannot afford to be without the teaching, prayer, worship and intercession that we were created for.

If the church in the city is going to be radically Christian, it will be a church that seeks at all costs to build unity with the whole body of Christ. Are our programmes so sacrosanct, or are we so busy that we dare not...

▷ invite ministers from other churches in the city to speak from our pulpit?

▷ set aside time regularly to visit other congregations and Christian organisations to see what they are doing?

▷ set up sister-church relationships so that every White suburban church is in direct relationship with a Black, Asian, Hispanic, Chinese, Cambodian, Vietnamese, or African congregation somewhere in the city?

▷ have families from other ethnic backgrounds in our homes for meals, and vice-versa?

▷ close down the Sunday services once a quarter so that our congregation can visit other congregations?

▷ build joint Sunday-school and youth programmes with other churches?

▷ adopt a small church and provide financial and human resources to enable that church to get established?

▷ make an appointment with one or more members of another church and go for a regular prayer-walk with them through the city?

▷ conduct joint missions conferences with several other churches so that we can share in one another's strengths and blessings together?

▷ bring boards of deacons or elders from different churches together just to build relationship and have fellowship in order to break down fears and mistrust?

▷ pray for other churches in the city on Sunday

mornings, from the pulpit, particularly those churches that we do not like or agree with theologically?

- ▷ conduct joint evangelistic outreaches at Christmas and Easter times?

Most likely you do not have time to participate in all these activities. But every Christian must take time for genuine fellowship that is characterised by accountability and honesty with other believers if he is to be a biblical Christian. It really boils down to a matter of obedience. If we are going to think and act Christianly then we must be willing to cut back on work and pleasure activities, demote the television and lead our family into meaningful friendship with other believers and our church community. As we make that commitment we will experience the authority promised us in Ephesians 2:6.

Does this kind of unity make a difference in the city? I know it does. In 1973 I arrived in the city of Amsterdam after a long trip through central Asia and Eastern Europe from Afghanistan. When I arrived in Amsterdam the thought came to me that I should pray for many other organisations, denominations and Christians to come to the city. This conviction grew as I began to visit local pastors and research the history of the church in the city. I could only find a handful of evangelical congregations, and it was obvious that Christians in the city were defeated, divided and discouraged.

We began to pray actively that God would bring church planters, pastors, prophets, evangelists, Christian workers, laymen and preachers out of retirement to the city. We focused our prayer on traditional churches and we prayed for new churches.

God richly answered our prayers. We have seen many pastors come out of retirement to accept the call to Dutch Reformed, Presbyterian and Baptist churches. New churches have been planted in neighbourhoods around the city, constituted not by church members changing congregations but by the unsaved coming to know Jesus Christ. Many Christian organisations have come to the city. We feel at one in heart and purpose with these pastors and organisations because we have prayed so much for them.

Some of them do not know the amount of time and prayer we have given to them. There was a period of several years where we prayed every noon hour for pastors and leaders by name. We would call ministers in the city and ask them what their prayer needs were. Some were shocked. Many of them were theologically liberal or unsaved. It made no difference to us. We were committed to praying for them.

The prayer paid off. Though we still have our problems, there is a healthy spirit of respect and love in the city of Amsterdam between Christian leaders. We have had joint celebrations in the city. We have gone on prayer-walks together. We have sent workers to one another and supported one another with finances and other resources. This kind of unity is possible and it does make a difference in the spiritual climate of the city.

*(7) Residence in the city*

The seventh category of spiritual weapons has to do with residence in the city. Whether in a suburb or a ghetto, whether in a neighbourhood populated by people from Asia or Mexico or the West Indies, whether in impersonal high-rise apartments, or tenement houses, or suburban-tract homes lined up wall to wall in a dehumanizing manner, God is calling Christians to lay down their aspirations and dreams of comfort and security, and commit themselves to God-directed residency within the city.

This is a biblical principle. Jesus is our example. He gave up his home. He gave up the comfort of heaven. He gave up the closeness of being with his Father. He gave up wealth and honour. He laid aside his divine rights in order that he might live among us.

If we are going to follow the example of the Lord Jesus, as we are commanded to do in the Scripture, then the basis of where we choose to live will not be what kind of equity it will bring in a house, or what kind of physical safety we judge it will provide us, but where God wants us. Spiritual warfare in this context means committing ourselves to a neighbourhood of people to demonstrate the gospel to them in word and deed. That means residency.

I challenge you to pray about moving out of your neighbourhood and moving into a neighbourhood of less economic status. Move to a neighbourhood of an ethnic minority group or lower economic status in order to learn from them and give to them of what God has put into your life. If you stay where you are, let it be because of calling, not comfort. (For a fuller discussion of this principle of residency, see chapter 6.)

Servant residency is not only where we live, but also involvement in the institutions and structures of the city. Residency means more than owning a house and driving back and forth to work. True residency means that we will follow the admonishment of Jeremiah writing to the exiles of Israel in the city of

Babylon, 'Seek the welfare of the city where I have sent you into exile, and pray to the Lord on its behalf, for in its welfare you will find your welfare' (Jeremiah 29:7). It means we will put our children in neighbourhood schools and get involved with parent-teacher organisations. It means that we will listen to the expressed needs of our neighbours and reflect that in the way we campaign and vote in local city elections. It means we will visit City Hall and let our voice be heard.

By repenting of overconsumption, rejecting fear and concern for our own well-being as a basis for deciding where to live, and responding to the challenge of servant residence, we are engaging ourselves in battle against spiritual powers that are determined to divide races and isolate Christians. Many neighbourhoods are constructed to protect the very cultural values that separate us. By refusing to adopt the aspirations of a security-conscious society, we are taking steps towards meaningful witness as Christians. This is not to say we cannot be witnesses to Christ if we live in 'nice' neighbourhoods, but it does mean we are willing to challenge spiritual strongholds that have kept many from Christ by overcoming personal fears and prejudices, turning aside from opportunities of financial gain, and living primarily to serve others.

By choosing to live in a run-down suburb or slum area, we are practising Christ's command to overcome evil with good. By responding in the opposite spirit to crime, violence, greed and fear, we are taking steps to conquer the powers. Yes, there is risk. Our children will get hassled at school, our home will be broken into and our well-patterned life will be disturbed. But if we do not step out of the comfort-zones we build around ourselves, can we say we have truly taken up our cross to follow Jesus?

There will be fears to conquer, if we do decide to live in the city. In the next two chapters, we'll be looking at the city from God's perspective, and allowing that to challenge our beliefs and some of our more serious misconceptions about the city.

# PART 2

# THE MEANING OF THE CITY

# CHAPTER 1

## *Looking for a City Built by God*

The incredulous look on the face of the farmer-turned-city-dweller said it all. His incredulity turned into a smile, almost laughter, as he settled down to hear me out. His resistance to what I was saying made it hard for me to concentrate. I was speaking to a group of suburban Christians, and was trying to share a different view about cities.

'The city is God's idea,' I declared. 'When he created Adam and Eve he intended them to have children, multiply in the garden, and populate Eden.'

Watching the dubious look on the faces of my audience, I carried on. 'When we think of a city we have images in our mind that are primarily negative, based on news reports of gang violence, drug wars, unemployed youth and homeless people. But try to imagine what the garden would have been like without sin. What if Adam and Eve had obeyed God?'

I tried to help my audience imagine what the garden would have been like without the Fall. If all the inhabitants of the Garden of Eden had obeyed God and had creatively and unselfishly supervised the natural resources at their disposal, what would have been the result? What kind of community would have developed had there been unity and harmony in their relationships and social interactions? As they grew in number a small city would have emerged, different from anything we know today.

When we think of cities we conjure up pictures of masses of humanity crowded into urban slum areas and inner city ghettos. We think of size—massive numbers of people and massive problems. But to put these problems into biblical perspective we must remember that God's original plan had to do with community, a covenant people gathered in a place to serve him. Without this understanding we will view modern-day 'city gatherings' negatively, based on the problems we see at hand. To understand the city biblically we must go back to God's original intention for mankind. Without this basis, we will have at best an incomplete view of the city, and at worst a warped and destructive theology of the city that leads to the total abandonment of the urban world.

The need for a theology for the city is urgent. If we believe cities are inherently evil, it will affect not only our attitudes towards the city, but also our understanding of the role of the church in modern society. Though the church should have developed an urban theology long ago out of a desire to understand God's mandate to 'multiply and fill the earth', we are now forced to respond because of the urbanisation of our planet. Cities can no longer be ignored.

Unfortunately, most definitions of the city are based on sociological interpretations of the city's function. While it is helpful to understand this perspective, it is more important to understand God's purpose in creating man with a longing for city 'togetherness'.

A Christian leader once commented to me, 'God created the earth, but it was man who made the city. It was the consequence of his rebellion against God that lead Cain to start the first city. This was a way of building his own society, showing that he did not need or want God. And that's how it's been ever since. Cities are the collecting places for sinful humanity and all our problems. Now Satan rules the cites because of man's sin.' With this view, it is no wonder that the church has had so little impact on the city. Many White, evangelical Christians despise the city.

I found out later that the farmer I mentioned above had lost everything he owned in a drought, and was forced to find employment in a nearby city. On the one hand he felt God had used his need for a job to bring him to the city, but on the other hand he felt the city was without hope and doomed to destruction. He tried to love the people around him, but felt he was in 'enemy territory' because of the inherent nature of the city, rather than the presence of principalities and powers as discussed in Chapter 1 above.

Many Christians live with this tension, feeling obligated to love the city but deeply disliking it. This tension has led some believers to spiritualise their reactions in order to justify their rejection of the city. They have developed a theology of escape, a view that says God is against the city and it is under his judgement. They see the city as a form of institutional evil. They have not only failed to seek out God's views on bringing people to the city, but also to respond with his love for the city-dweller. Much of our evangelical 'sub'-urban lifestyle is tainted with this pessimism and callousness towards the city. But rather than emotionally react to cities because of their problems, we should consider them in the light of God's intended purpose as the gathering place of his covenant people.

Just like the individuals that inhabit them, cities are fallen. Though they take on a life and power of their own, a city is people, a group of individuals. Therefore they have worth and value to God both as individuals *and as a community*. Just as we have learned that we are significant and valuable to the Lord even though we have sinned against him, so whole communities have a place in God's plan. Just as we have learned that it is important to love the neediest person because they are created in God's image, so we must learn to love the neediest city for the same reason.

Without a biblical theology of the city we will succumb to the prevailing pessimism around us. We will develop a hopelessness that will undermine our love and faith for the city. A state of unbelief towards the city already permeates the church, and obviously undercuts our mandate to be salt and light in society.

God intends the church to have a role of moral and spiritual leadership in modern society. If the primary attitude towards the city is negative, how can the church provide such leadership, located outside the city itself? You cannot lead someone you do not like; the very nature of spiritual leadership is based on love and relationship.

The most powerful influence the church can have on society is through prayer. But without a biblical perspective on the city, our prayers will be filled with unbelief.

Obviously we will never develop a personal love for the city if we believe it is *inherently* evil, rather than corrupted by principalities and powers. Without a change of theology concerning the city we will continue to hold our suburban and rural lifestyles as sacrosanct. We will rationalise our flight from the city with pious concerns about our family, when all the time our real motivation was fear and selfishness.

## Built by God

God planned our corporate existence. We can know with certainty that he wanted us to gather together in city-communities because he created us to be social beings. The Lord made this abundantly clear in the opening pages of the Bible when he commanded Adam and Eve to multiply and fill the earth: 'So God created man in his own image—male and female he created them.... And God said to them, "Be fruitful and multiply, and fill the earth, and subdue it"' (Genesis 1:27–28).

The longing for 'togetherness' created in us is tapped when we experience meaningful fellowship with other believers. But that is to be a starting point, not the sum total of its meaning. We are to go on from there to be God's people in the place where we live, providing a taste of true love and joy through touching other people's lives around us.

Knowing this, we have a biblical point of reference in which to consider cities today. They are among the places he intends us to live together, expressing our various cultures, and living out our commitments to fulfil his plan for our lives: 'he made from one every nation of men to live on all the face of the earth, having determined ... the boundaries of their habitation, that they should seek God' (Acts 17:26–27). Cities are part of God's boundaries for our habitation, and help to fulfil his sovereign purpose that we seek him.

It is amazing how much we believe in the sovereignty of God but how much we resist the idea that the city is God's creation. God can do anything, it seems, as long as we approve! Not only did God intend Adam and Eve to plant a city in a garden, he has continued to call cities into being. The Bible states clearly that God draws up the 'boundaries of man's habitation' (Acts 17:26). He is actively fulfilling his original plan to bring people together to fulfil his purposes. And that means cities—large and small.

Does this mean everyone 'must' live in a city? The question misses the point. The size of a city should not be the determining factor in our decision about where to live, nor should the social climate or value of property. Where does God want me? Where will my life count most for him? How best can I serve him in a place? What is on his heart for a community? These are the questions kingdom people should be asking.

Large cities are nothing more than a collection of various communities, networks of people if you wish, brought together in one place. Realistically, we cannot effectively serve more than one of the networks or communities of people in a given city. So the focus for finding God's will should not be the 'largeness' or 'niceness' of a place, but the 'rightness' of those whom we are called to serve and live among.

While a small 'town' may be said to have a single cultural ethos and sense of community, cities contain cultural, ethno-linguistic and sociological networks or people-groups. We must learn to think in terms of peoplehood, not place; of serving, not circumstances. Most White, Western Christians are very ethnocentric. They stick to their own kind, blind to the new realities: God is shaking up the world. The city is being used by God to bring peoples to each other and to himself.

Though living together in the city exposes man's sinfulness, this does not mean that God had nothing to do with creating 'city'. His plans were good—it is man who fell, not God. And it is still God's love that brings people together in cities. God could sovereignly stop the world-wide urbanisation that is taking place, but he has not done so. I urge you not to view the rapid urbanisation of our planet and your nation as a 'sign of the times' but to see it as our loving Father seeking to bring his creation together in order that they might rediscover his purpose for their lives.

If people refuse to submit to God, then in his love for them he will use the pressure of being together with other selfish people to reveal their need of him. God has not turned back from his purpose for our lives. Nothing can deter him. The city is one more way that he is using to accomplish his will.

Christians are the ones who seem to be most resistant to God urbanising the world. Perhaps the spirit of worldliness has entered the hearts of believers more than we realise. When the first criterion for making decisions is, 'Will it make me happy, secure and comfortable?' something has gone desperately wrong in the church. Do we believe that God would dare ask us to sacrifice what we want in order to serve him?

The purpose of developing an urban theology is not just to respond to the pessimism and anti-urban prejudice found among most Christians, but to help us respond obediently to God. We cannot escape the city. It is the dominant social force of twentieth-century life, and it is the plan and purpose of our sovereign God.

The Bible is an eschatological book, recording God's purposes for all of human history. The making and remaking of this world begins and ends within the first and last pages of the Bible. Between its covers, the Bible unfolds God's redemptive plan for the whole creation.

The fact that history ends in a city, the new Jerusalem, gives us greater clarity over how it was intended to begin. The eschatological picture of the people of God gathered around the throne in the new Jerusalem reveals to us God's eternal purpose for his creation. The marriage feast of the Lamb in the heavenly city speaks of the celebration that God wants when his creation gathers together, not only for eternity, but right now.

Having begun this planet with those purposes, God has not changed his mind. Through urbanisation, the redemptive heart of God is at work drawing his creation back to himself. If we do not love cities we are missing out on his redemptive work on this planet.

### A biblical definition of the city

What is a city? We should define the city in accordance with God's purposes for our corporate existence as revealed in the Bible. I suggest the following definition:

> The city is *people* created by God, gathered together to serve him and live for his glory. It is also the *place* where his people are called to be stewards over the resources and environment of his creation, living in peace with one another, and submitting to just magistrates who govern according to God's laws.

According to Dutch city planner Pieter Bos, there are several vital elements in such a definition. The first is 'people'. A 'gathered people' is a community, with all the responsibilities any civilised, much less Christian, community has towards God and one another. Like Abraham of old, we long for a city 'whose builder and maker is God' (Hebrews 11:10). This longing for 'togetherness' is planted deep within us by God. It is our destiny to be together for eternity, and that longing manifests itself in the here and now by wanting love, friendship, marriage, companionship and Christian fellowship.

The second element in our definition is 'place'. We will discuss this in greater detail later (Chapter 6), so it will suffice to say here that God chooses places for his people to gather. This means incarnation. It means we invest ourselves, create residency, put down our roots, with the intention to give to the place God has called us.

Still another important dimension of our definition of the city is stewardship. God gave Adam and Eve dominion over the earth, not to use it up as quickly as possible (which our economies of growth seem to imply), but to rule over it wisely, so that it is used in a godly fashion. Surely the problem of urban pollution and smog (of which suburban commuters are major contributors—we must remember that the next time we are abhorred by the 'dirty inner city') is a reminder that we have failed miserably in this regard.

Another dimension of the definition of the city is harmonious relationships. When we are told by well-meaning people that Christians should stay out of politics because it is the role of the church to deal with spiritual matters, we face a dilemma. It is God's will that races live in harmony with one another, and that the rich should not exploit the poor. When these sins exist in society, the church must speak up. We cannot be silent because someone feels that 'getting involved in politics' is none of our business. We must not be silent in the face of sin, whether it be the sins of an individual or an entire city. God is a God of justice. The city is God's idea—he has fashioned it and determined its purpose. Therefore, everything that happens in the city is of vital importance to the concerned Christian.

Lastly, a city is to have God-fearing magistrates who govern righteously. When that happens it bodes good for the citizens of the city. But when there is corruption, injustice, power-seeking and political manoeuvering, the city will not fulfil its God-given purpose.

## The sacred place

The earth is the Lord's—including the city. There is much evidence of urban theology in the Bible. A clear urban tradition is found throughout the Scriptures that is both positive in nature and points to God's esteem for the places where he calls his people. This tradition of the 'sacred place' as Ray Bakke calls it (*The Urban Christian*, p. 63) assures us that where God's people are, he is in their midst.

In the Old Testament, men of God often built altars to remember the great things God did for them in a particular place. Sometimes this was because of answered prayer, other times it was because of victories in battle, and on other occasions it was because of unique spiritual experiences. God's people were not afraid to look upon those special places as sacred. Jacob regarded the place of his dream in the desert as holy. He called it Bethel—Hebrew for 'house of God.'

We can look upon any place as holy, including the most impersonal suburb, ungodly office environment or poorest neighbourhood. They are equally important to the Lord. This means Calcutta is sacred to the Lord, as is New York, Melbourne, Liverpool and Belfast. If we abhor these places, it is more a reflection on us than on the city.

## Mrs London

God's concern is not only for individuals, but also for groups of people. He calls and makes covenants with families, tribes and nations. His covenants with Noah, Abraham, and David and their descendants testify to the unique love God has for 'peoples' which he has brought into being.

It is typical of people from post-industrial, Western cultures to look at the rest of the world through individualistic eyes, rather than seeing extended families and peoples. This is reflected in the lack of distinction between the singular and plural 'you' in our modern English language. The result is an uphill battle to perceive our calling to covenant 'peoplehood'. We interpret promises in the Bible that were given to the body of Christ and the nation of Israel very privately.

Because of these tendencies, we miss the significance of those portions of Scripture that speak to cities as personalities. Judgement is often pronounced on whole cities, and not on particular individuals in them. Cities are often described as having personal (female) characteristics. In Ezekiel 16 Jerusalem is condemned for her 'sins' and the prophet goes on to refer to her 'sisters' Sodom and Samaria.

Blessings are also pronounced on entire cities. In Jeremiah 29:7 the exiles in Babylon are told to 'seek the welfare of the city'. It was not particular individuals they were told to bless, but the city as a whole. God saw the city collectively, addressing 'her' need for being cared for in this amazing passage of collective grace.

This commitment to the whole city is very dynamic in the book of Isaiah. In Isaiah 61 the prophet refers to the Lord's plans for the renewed city, a dream which is to be consummated in the new Jerusalem. This is the city that Jesus weeps for many years later, and speaks to prophetically when he prophesies to her of her collective spiritual blindness (Luke 19:41–43). In Isaiah 60 the Lord promises 'her' that her walls will be built up and kings shall minister to her.

A city takes on a spiritual life of her own. The city is something that is more than the sum of her individuals. The prophecies concerning Damascus, Philistia, Tyre, Edom and Moab in the book of Amos are warnings to us that we cannot turn a blind eye to the spiritual state of the city in which we live. We cannot flee our responsibility by moving to another part of the city, or leaving it altogether.

The spiritual and historical backgrounds of a city are interrelated. Just as the actions of the past influence the street prostitute to take up her trade, so the past actions of people in the city influence the city's spiritual development. And just as a raped woman struggles for acceptance, a city plundered by unrighteous merchants will bear the marks of the injustice in her corporate psyche.

## Who is responsible for the city?

Over and over again cities are referred to as corporate entities, with personalities and a spiritual character that the people of God in that city are held responsible for (Ezekiel 27; Zephaniah 2:15; Revelation 18:7; and chapters 2 and 3 of Revelation).

It is not the architecture of the buildings that give a

city her personality and spiritual state, but the collective decisions of the people in the city. It was not the presence of unrighteous people that finally brought destruction on Sodom, but the absence of ten righteous men. And it was the sins of robbery, injustice and violence that brought the judgement of the Lord against Samaria (Amos 3). The decisions of merchant organisations and city councils, as well as the collective morality of the people, is what turns a loose-knit group of people into a legal and spiritual body.

## God has plans for the city

It is also true that if cities have collective personalities, it is possible for them to do justice collectively. The central role that Jerusalem played in the spiritual history of Israel speaks to the plans that God sets in motion for whole cities. This is confirmed when we study the role of the cities of refuge in the Old Testament. God wanted to use these cities, that is, the collective citizenry and their appointed magistrates, to serve those who needed protection in society.

God intended the cities of the land of Canaan to be a blessing and not a curse. Deuteronomy 6:10 speaks of 'great and goodly cities....' Cities served different purposes for the children of Israel, including storehouse cities, cities of defence, and spiritual centres of renewal and spiritual blessing (Numbers 35:1–34; 2 Chronicles 8:5–6; 11:5; Deuteronomy 16:18; Psalm 72:16; and Proverbs 11).

## Mrs London is fallen

Sadly, sin has spoiled God's plan for cities. Cain built the first city after Adam and Eve aborted God's purposes in the garden, and called it Enoch, meaning 'my beginning'. The tendency to independence and pride in cities is self-evident. But this has not always been the case. Some evangelists have experienced responses from entire cities to the preaching of the gospel. Charles Finney, George Whitefield and Evan Roberts saw great moves of God in cities. What Jonah experienced in Nineveh was certainly no small thing.

Throughout the Old Testament, kings established their power by building cities to glorify themselves and their empires. This feeds into Satan's scheme to corrupt God's urban plans. 'Kill the sons of the king of Babylon,' cries the prophet Isaiah (Isaiah 14:21), 'lest they cover the earth with their cities.'

Modern cities tend to be more pluralistic and culturally diverse. It is as if there are many villages from different nations and cultures piled on top of each other. This complicates both the spiritual nature of cities and the process of bringing the good news of the gospel. Modern cities are impossible to reach without the help of God. One of the most tragic mistakes the church can make is to fail to discern the complex and diverse spiritual personality of modern cities.

Strategies for mass evangelism must be decentralised if they are to be effective. The gospel must be taken to 'peoples' rather than expecting them to come to us. We must go in the languages of the peoples of the city, and in culturally sensitive methods. Incarnation and proclamation must never be separated in the city—or the consequences are tragic.

Pieter Bos, architect and city planner, and now a missionary in Amsterdam, says, 'In modern cities decisions are often made haphazardly and with no regard for God. As a result, the city falls under the influence of the principalities and powers of Satan. Satan uses the anonymous nature of the city as an environment which encourages the growth of evil. People flock to the cities seduced by the lie that there they will survive. The results are evident in the environment, in the economy, in social problems and in resistance to the gospel' (*City Cries*, p. 4).

Though intended by God to serve his purposes, cities are fallen. Unfortunately, most Christians believe that cities are a necessary evil. Tolerate them if you must, and avoid them if you can. Most of us believe God created man, and man created the city. Following this logic, the very existence of cities is a fruit of the Fall, a result of man's rebellion against God and therefore inherently evil. According to this view, Satan is the rightful ruler over the cities, not God. But this is not substantiated by Scriptures. This view is more laden with sociological pessimism than biblical insight.

Cities are no more intrinsically evil that man is. Though mankind is sinful by nature, he is created in the image of God. The same is true for what we call cities. Though their present form is marred by personal and corporate sin, it is God who created man for community, and community for man.

Just as we are called to love fallen men and women with the love of God, we should love and respect the city. We should see the city for who she was intended to be, and not just for what we think she has become. I say 'what we think she has become' because all too often our fear of urban life is far worse than reality. Moreover, there is a tendency to develop an evangelical subculture that baptises certain values and lifestyles and calls them holy, when they are nothing more than expressions of our own selfishness, fear and cultural myopia.

## Redeeming the city

So far I have said that the city is God's idea, that he intends the city to be a blessing and not a curse, that cities have collective personalities and spiritual characters of their own, that the evil character of a city develops because of the individual and corporate choices men make, and that believers are responsible for the spiritual well-being of their city.

When we compare what the Bible says about God's purpose for cities, and what is happening in many cities today, we can draw two conclusions: there is a tremendous spiritual battle being fought for control of the city, and many Christians have abandoned the city. Not all Christians, I must point out. For many believers, the city is home. Asians, Blacks, Hispanics, all have embraced the city and celebrate its life daily.

What is the implication of these truths for Christians? Though there are many, three stand out with particular importance and urgency. First, we must repent of our urban prejudices and cultivate God's love in our heart for the city. This will not come without prayer, and repentance for any lack of love for the city. And it will not grow without personal involvement with people in the city. Love will not grow without relationship. Are you prepared to get involved in genuine friendship with people in the city? Have them in your home? Visit theirs?

Secondly, through intercession and listening to God, through research and study, and through listening to God's people who are already in the city, we must discern God's unique role for the city we live in. By studying the spiritual history of our city, and by looking carefully at what God's people are presently doing, we can gain a sense of perspective and appreciation for the continuity of God's work in the place he has called us. We are not stepping into a spiritual vacuum. God has been at work, and by discerning what he has been doing among his people through the years, we can develop greater understanding of what is on his heart for the city in which we live.

And last, Christians and church leaders must provide servant leadership to the city. By loving the city, being involved in its daily affairs, calling it into account for its unrighteousness, proclaiming the gospel, participating in its institutions and affirming its strengths, Christians begin to fulfil Christ's mandate to be in the world but not of the world.

Many evangelical Christians do not see the big picture. They do not think in terms of the overall spiritual climate of the city, what cultural and spiritual forces are at work that mitigate for and against the gospel, what role the institutions of the city play in its corporate character, and what God has been doing historically in that place.

We Christians do not take ourselves seriously enough. Our role is to be more than spectator prophets, coming out of our spiritual closets on occasion to march against pornography and campaigning for or against the latest political gurus, only to disappear until we get sufficiently riled up over another issue. We have an ongoing and significant role that can be fulfilled or failed, but never denied. We are God's covenant people, gathered by himself to serve the city, to be stewards over the resources of the city, to bring peace to the city, to prophesy to the city and to lead it in righteousness and justice.

## CHAPTER 2

# *Urban Myths and Biblical Realities*

**Myth** n. **1.** One of the fictions or half-truths forming part of the ideology and values of a society. **2.** A notion based more on tradition or convenience than on fact. **3.** A traditional story originating in a pre-literate society dealing with supernatural beings. **4.** Any real or fictional, recurring theme that appeals to the consciousness of a people by embodying its cultural ideals or by giving expression to deep, commonly felt emotions. **5.** Any fictitious or imaginary story, explanation, person or thing.

**Urban myths 1.** Nature is closer to God. **2.** The city is impersonal. **3.** Cities are crime-ridden and dangerous. **4.** The city is not a safe place to raise children. **5.** The city cannot be changed.

This century has been characterised as the century of revolution, the century of war, of globalisation, and of information; perhaps we will even be called the century of achievement if we do not destroy ourselves first. But nothing we have done as the human race has so universally affected our lives as the decision to flock together in cities in such great numbers.

The city is the most dominant sociological force in this century. The seriousness of our Christian commitment will be judged by our response to the city and the challenges it presents to us.

There are several reasons on a human level why so many people have migrated to cities: employment, education, escape from famine and starvation, and if we are more fortunate than most, to enjoy wealth and achievements. That mankind has flocked to the city with such speed and in such great numbers is what is so remarkable.

## The century of the city

By the year 2000, 650 million people will live in the 60 largest cities of the world. In 1980 there were about 175 cities each with a population exceeding one million. In 1989 there were 348. That number will swell to almost 500 by the end of the century.

Over 450 million people have moved to cities since 1945, and according to UN estimates, another 500 million will flood cities in the last decade of this century. Humankind is changing with breathtaking speed into an urban species. UN demographers characterise the movement as 'the greatest mass migration in human history'.

It is estimated that in 1900 one in twenty people worldwide dwelt in a city. Today, one in two people live in cities, and by the year 2020, three out of four people will be urban inhabitants.

These numbers help us grasp the reality of the urbanisation of the planet, but very few of us have stopped to think through the implications that such rapid social change means for our lives personally. We know what we don't like about the city, but that can be a very superficial reaction. We must go beyond our personal fears and feelings and think of the city in terms of God's plan for the nations.

In the preceding chapter, I tried to lay a biblical foundation for looking at the city through God's eyes. To go further, it is necessary to examine the prejudices we have against the city. Prejudice is always rooted in a stereotype, which results not only in fear and rejection, but in believing a lie. Believing a lie, or a myth, justifies our actions, at least to ourselves.

Are there truths in our stereotypes? Most definitely, but they are often half-truths and generalisations shaped by one or two limited experiences or an unforgiven incident. Many of our prejudices are inherited from our parents, and then reinforced by our own limited contact with people we mistrust.

The truth about ourselves and our myths will be found by carefully examining all sides of a thing, then drawing objective conclusions. More importantly, truth is found by seeing people and situations from God's perspective. What looks good and acceptable to a calloused sinner takes on a different perspective when a person is broken by God's love.

To see the city as God sees it is not merely an intellectual exercise. And to explode the myths that have justified our reticence to embrace the city with God's love will require more than reading a book or hearing a sermon. There must be ruthless pursuit of truth on our knees. The ground of our heart must be broken up so that we can be in the right state to receive spiritual insight from the Lord.

I am compelled to ask if you are truly committed to such an exercise.

## Pulling down idols in our minds

A myth can quickly become an idol, a spiritual hiding place. It can become holy to us, something we will not and cannot let go. Like the myths of old, our personal myths can become objects of veneration. They become like gods to us. They occupy a place of such importance that they are more important than God himself. An idol is anything that takes God's place. A myth about the city becomes an idol in our heart when it prevents us from loving the city with God's love and being anxious to do whatever the Lord wants us to do to serve the city.

When we cannot hear and obey God's voice to love the city and live in it because of enslavement to false values and ungodly fears, we have become slaves to our idols. It is in that state that myths take root in our hearts. We believe them in order to justify our disobedience.

The problems of the city run contrary to the doctrine that God wants all Christians to be financially successful and materially prosperous. These doctrines undermine sacrifice and make it very difficult for Christians to lay down their lives for the sake of others.

We will examine some of our Christian myths in this chapter. I will try to do so in a manner that is objective; there are elements of truth in our urban myths. We want to acknowledge the very real problems of our great cities, and find the biblical realities.

One only needs to examine the consequences of our urban myths to realise their harmfulness: fear, despair, abandonment, paralysis of action, separation of believers and millions of people suffering without practical or spiritual help. Let's look at some of the more prevalent myths that have been used to justify the church's retreat from the city.

## Myth Number One: Nature is closer to God than the city

Harvie Conn points out that in one survey it was found that 91·4% of all evangelical Christians in the United States live outside large cities of one million or more (*A Clarified Vision for Urban Mission*, p. 17). The vision of the church in that nation and its role in society is being shaped by rural and suburban theologians. It is no wonder that it is so difficult to recruit urban missionaries from America or to stimulate evangelical involvement in the inner cities. Though this statistic may not apply to the UK, Australia and other Western countries in exactly the same percentages, the desire to escape the city and find comfort in materialism is, it seems to me, the same.

This has not always been the case. During the Middle Ages, Western cities were associated with freedom and self-determination. During the Enlightenment, cities became centres of culture and learning. Conn points out that the formation of the English language reflects this flattering but passing view of the city. I borrow a quote from his book:

> We city dwellers, at least in ancient days, were supposed to be more civil in our manners and more civilized in our ways than others, for both of these words, *civil and civilized*, are the eventual children of the Latin term *civis* which meant 'one who lives in the city'. All city folks, you see, were regarded as automat-

> ically cultured and housebroken. And from the ancient Latin we have borrowed the word *urbs* which also meant city, and we used it to create the word *urbane* which describes the smooth manners that were presumed to be characteristic of metropolitan society.... And from the Greek *polis*, 'city', we inherited our word politic. If you are politic, you are expedient, shrewd, discreet, and artful in your address and your procedure, which sounds dangerously like a city slicker!

But eighteenth-century industrialisation led to urban growth, and problems of poverty and labour exploitation became rampant. People began to fear the city, and came to look upon it as the cause rather than the location of the problems.

The city became a symbol in people's minds of social disorder and sin. That picture has grown to mythic proportions. Superficial news reports are broadcast nightly into our homes, confirming our worst fears. The 'News' is bad news and it is all about the city.

It is only one step further to build a theology of escape: what we see happening in the city is evil, therefore the city is evil. And the Bible says we should avoid all appearance of evil, so we run from the city. But what we think we see is not always the truth. Cities are like people, and complex problems cannot be dealt with by superficial generalisations.

Some theologians believe that the children of Israel were nomads, and only after the time of Solomon did they as a people attempt to build the first city. The implication is clear: when Solomon lost his wisdom through sexual corruption, the same spirit was spread throughout the land. The people of God lusted after the pleasures of the flesh, like their king. And it was this lust that led to the first cities being constructed by the children of Israel.

Such a theological construction is appealing to some. The only problem is that it does not fit the biblical realities. In fact, when the children of Israel were entering the Promised Land, in Deuteronomy 6:10–12 God 'encouraged them to see the cities they would now occupy as gifts from Him' (Conn, page 57).

In the United States this myth is linked to the American Dream. That dream is built on a vision of God's blessing, which is manifested in material abundance. Americans know God has blessed them because 'we are the richest nation on the face of the earth'. But the problems of the city threaten that dream, and they are inconsistent with the doctrine of prosperity.

It is this vision of materialistic Christianity that has alienated the working classes of Britain, Central Europe, Australia and the United States. This kind of superficiality is despised by the revolutionaries of South America who have become embittered because of the injustices of the wealthy towards the poor. Sadly, it is inconceivable to most Americans that many people do not admire their materialism.

One African brother challenged the concept that materialism and wealth are a valid measure of God's blessing in a developed society. 'Look what your materialism has done for you. It has made you soft. You have lost your simplicity, your ability to sacrifice. Your children have turned to drugs and your families are breaking up. I am not against material benefits, but if you are a developed society, I don't want what you are developed into.'

God does bless people and prosper them. Hard work, honesty and righteous living results in upward mobility. But baptising materialism in the name of Jesus, endorsing competition without reckoning with the sinful nature of man, and sanctifying unending economic growth without restraint is not only unbiblical, it has hindered us from serving the urban poor and made our witness a sham in the eyes of those committed to justice in this world. It has robbed many believers of their vision for world evangelisation. It has turned scores of evangelical and charismatic churches inward on themselves. Many pastors have lost their passion for the lost. They are still waiting for easy church growth, forgetting that it is God's sovereign blessing and not some spiritual secret that brings people to their churches.

We have forgotten that where *God* is, there is the blessing. His presence is more important than anything we do. Any place God visits with his presence is holy, because he is in the midst of the people in that place. He is in the midst of West Indian churches in the big cities of Great Britain. He is in the midst of Italian and Greek communities in the Western suburbs of Melbourne, Australia. He is in the midst of the Maoris in Auckland, New Zealand and the Turkish guest workers in Frankfurt, West Germany. The city is holy because *God is in the city.*

Many of us are blinded by our cultural prejudices. We think everyone wants to be in a suburb or the countryside. The Chinese culture is an example of a people that do not aspire to rural lifestyles. They feel far more secure and at home when they are crowded close together in the city. God has created all peoples different, and to presume that 'our' way is the best way is the worst kind of spiritual and ethnic pride.

Some people love the open countryside, and others get charged up in the city. I love both. I was delighted when a few years ago our children fell in love with the bustle of Amsterdam life. When people asked them if they wanted to live in the countryside, our kids thought they were crazy. They love living in the city.

Even though I grew up fishing and hunting and love the outdoors, if I had to live *all* my life in a mountain cabin it would be a death sentence. Our family owns a home in the mountains, and we love to use it for family retreats, but my heart is in the city. That is where the action is. That is where the people are. I come alive in the city. I love to walk its streets. I love the hustle and bustle, the political activity, the museums and sidewalk cafés. I don't just love the city with the love of the Lord; I like the city. It refuels me to walk its streets.

To me it is just not true that you have to leave the city to get spiritually refreshed. Don't misunderstand me, I need times of rest and retreat like anyone else. But I have no illusions about the countryside being more spiritual than the city. It is God's presence that draws people to himself, not our geographical location. God is with his people in the city and in the rural areas. He created nature and he created man for community. Both are from the Lord, and both can be destroyed or enjoyed by man.

**Myth Number Two: The city is impersonal**

Cities can be overwhelming. Riding the underground train in New York, London, Bombay, or Paris, or fighting throngs of people in Hong Kong,

Los Angeles or Sydney, can be a staggering experience. The same feeling occurs when one drives past street after street of tenement blocks and high-rise apartment buildings in any major city in the world. After staying in India for several weeks, my wife Sally described it as 'Christmas rush crowds all year long'.

Cities bombard people with overwhelming sensory input. Sounds, sights and smells all combine to overload our sensory gates. For the newcomer to the city this can be a very intimidating experience. It seems too much for any person to handle. Psychological studies have shown that when this occurs people tend to narrow their psychological focus, withdrawing into themselves to shut out unwanted input.

Thus, the bus and underground passenger retreats into his own world of reading material or lost thoughts as he rides shoulder to shoulder with a hundred fellow commuters. And the person living in a tiny flat in London avoids his nearby neighbours. It is emotional survival.

The perception of the average Christian is that all this sensory input produces mass loneliness. Millions of faceless people busily running to and fro, without any human contact. It is not hard to understand why spiritually minded people see this as a negative phenomenon. We worry about city dwellers, wondering if they are hiding in the city and if anyone has ever shared the gospel with them, much less become personally involved in their lives.

That is the perception, but do we have all the facts? Do our conclusions accurately describe the universal realities, or are they generalisations? In fact, has this view of the city become a myth that we have accepted, the result of which is an unhealthy and unbiblical despair towards the city? Let's take a look at some facts that will help us get a more balanced view of big city living.

**(1)** Loneliness is a relative thing. Not everyone in the city is lonely. Many people love the big city, and have developed a network of friendships with people of their own language, cultural affinity and/or neighbourhood.

Harvie Conn reminds us that mass migrations from Europe to the United States and Australia in the last century led to the formation of voluntary associations of all kinds. Groups were formed to assist the newcomer on the block with language learning, medical aid, ethnic consciousness, political awareness and church attendance.

Whole neighbourhoods of Italian, Greek and Irish people emerged, and in some places still remain. The same is true today of Cambodian and Vietnamese refugees in Paris, Houston and Los Angeles. The return of Pakistanis, Indians and West Indians to Britain is referred to as the phenomenon of the 'empire striking back'. And they are not alone. They have formed the same sort of clubs and associations within their own community in order to adjust to their new environs.

The fact that crowdedness in the city is perceived as impersonal tells us more about those who feel that way than those who live in the city. White, upper-middle-class suburbanites view the city through their own cultural prejudices. They fail to recognise the differences between cultures, or the difference between culture and Christian values, and react accordingly. While single-family dwellings and lots of land and open space are seen by some as natural and necessary, working-class populations and those of different ethnic backgrounds regard the facts differently.

Conn points out that 'contact with others is positive, a sign of belonging, not a sign of crowding. Inner-city children are more comfortable being with others than being alone' (Conn, p. 45).

There are many lonely people in the suburbs too. Moving out of the city isn't the solution to loneliness!

**(2)** Urban life has not produced monolithic loneliness. Many people, particularly the poor, enjoy being close to their family and friends. Those who work with urban slum dwellers soon learn that for the poor, joy is found in their friendships; though poor in material things they are rich in relationships. It is only natural for a person with these kinds of values to want to be close to those they love.

Christian workers in Manila's 'smokey mountain' have been amazed to watch those who were offered opportunity to move off the smouldering garbage mountain turn down better living conditions to remain close to their friends.

While city-dwelling Europeans appear to be unfriendly to the American tourist, Americans are seen as superficial: friendly to everyone, but here today and gone tomorrow. 'Cold' European city dwellers take longer to make friends, but their friendships are for life. They may appear to be lonely to the casual observer, but in reality they often have deep friendships which they focus on almost exclusively.

Amsterdam's three hundred or more 'brown cafés' are patronised by 'regulars' who obviously enjoy one another's company. They talk openly of their problems to those they know. One bar-tending couple told me that, though they lost money in their café, they kept it open because they would miss their friends too much if they closed down.

**(3)** The city is not necessarily anonymous in nature to those who live in it. Harvey Cox tells in his book *The Secular City* that many people moved to the city to escape the lack of anonymity of the village. They were seeking opportunities to build relationships based on free choice and not the forced geographical proximity of the village (Conn, page 43).

In the nation of Holland, village life can be quite harsh due to the heavy legalism of hyper-Calvinistic churches that dominate village life. In that nation at least, many urban dwellers have moved to the city to find an escape from stifling religious intolerance.

People in high-rise apartments may not know their neighbours, but this does not mean they do not have relationships. They may be living where they are to maintain their privacy, just as farmers in some rural areas don't want to get too 'close' to their neighbours—who happen to live three miles down the road.

**(4)** City-life does not cause emotional problems. Some urban sociologists believe the size of the city eats away at mental health, creating 'urban malaise'—loneliness, depression and anxiety. An in-depth study of Manhattan residents points the other way:

> Some 1,660 New Yorkers were questioned in the 1950s; 695 of the same group were surveyed again in the 1970s. The results? The mental health of New Yorkers was slightly better than that of the country residents. In fact, the mental health had improved dramatically over the interval between the two samples, especially for women. A survey taken later by the National Center for Health Statistics reinforced the conclusion. The survey sought to find the incidence of stress-related, chronic health problems, such as hypertension and heart disease, among people over sixty-

five. It disclosed such problems in 47·8 per 100 farm residents, 47·5 for small-town residents, and 40·5 for city residents. (Conn, p. 45.)

Behaviour is not a problem of geography, nor does the city create an impersonal environment, although it can contribute to a person's emotional needs if they do not build meaningful friendships. There is not something inherently evil about the city that induces problems or brings out the worst in people. City is community, and it will reflect what the people make of it themselves, just as a small village can vary in its spiritual make-up according to the character of the people.

**Myth Number Three: Cities are crime-ridden and dangerous**

There is crime in the large cities of every Western nation. No one denies this reality, except those involved in breaking the law. But the reaction to crime on the part of Christians is out of all proportion to the facts.

Crime statistics change from neighbourhood to neighbourhood, and given the large and sprawling nature of our cities, it seems that one must judge each suburb, township, and neighbourhood on its own merits.

Further, the definition of crime must also be examined. Certain types of crimes are more prevalent in certain areas, and others are common to all environments. Child abuse, chemical dependency and tax evasion are found everywhere. 'White-collar crimes' such as embezzlement and computer crime are concentrated in middle-class neighbourhoods. If the white-collar criminal was treated equally in the justice systems of Western nations the perception that crime is concentrated in the poorer areas of the city would change. The suburbs would be seen to have more than their share of criminal activity.

We tend to define crime in terms of what we perceive to be a threat to our well-being, such as mugging and break-ins. Such limited definitions of crime are overlaid with racial fears. This kind of limited perspective not only produces a myth of suburban safety and inner-city danger, but perpetuates inequality and racism in society.

Many third-world and European cities are extremely safe. While certain neighbourhoods do have some physical danger, most are free of violent crimes. Other wealthier neighbourhoods are filled with the dangers not so easily seen, such as sexual immorality, crass materialism and selfish ambition.

Westerners tend to look at all cities through coloured glasses. They impute the fear of their cities to all the other cities in the world. Very few societies in the world are as violent as the United States or Great Britain. Perhaps the real problem in the States is that it was birthed as a nation in a violent manner. This violent spirit seems to permeate every aspect of the culture.

I am writing as an American citizen. I see no prospect of change in my home nation until there is national repentance over pride in the American revolution and the violent manner in which the country insisted on its right to nationhood and sovereignty. If I understand the United States properly, the importance of American independence from the British is more a middle-class value for white Americans than something Hispanics or Blacks get excited about.

The false perception that violent crime is only an

inner-city problem in the United States is exposed in an incident where a gang of youths went through Central Park in New York City 'mauling'. They beat one young finance executive until she was unconscious, but not before brutally raping her over and over again. An inner-city crime problem? Follow-up investigations revealed that these were not drug-dependent youths from poor parts of the city, but bored kids from middle- and upper-income homes out for a 'good time'. Violence is not the domain of the poor.

Even when there are problems of violence in neighbourhoods, the challenge to followers of Christ is one of taking our commitment wholly to follow the Lord Jesus. Did we give our lives totally to him or not?

In the final analysis, it should make no difference to the true believer if a place is dangerous or not. Our first concern should not be for our own life. Nor should it be for how much equity we can build up in our house. If you have given your life completely to the Lord Jesus, then it is time to stop complaining and backing out on your commitment. God is looking for those who will give up their rights, lay down their lives, and follow him. Anywhere, any time. No excuses, no exceptions.

### Myth Number Four: The city is not a safe place to raise children

Raising kids is a challenge no matter where it is done. The responsibility of being a good parent is an awesome one, and not to be taken lightly. Kids face so many pressures growing up, complicating that process by living in a challenging neighbourhood seems foolhardy. Or is it?

Raising one's children in an inner-city neighbourhood or an urban slum area is not an easy task. To do so requires the grace of God. Having said that, anyone who has a healthy family and a solid relationship with the Lord is a candidate for the Lord's calling. God wants normal people to take up that call. Millions of families are already doing so without the luxury of a choice in the matter.

There is a common Christian myth that has prevented many people from obeying God when it comes to his calling on their families. It goes something like this:

> To be a good parent I must provide the *best* for my children. They must attend a good Christian school, wear fashionable clothes so their friends will like them, and they must have the best home we can afford, in a nice neighbourhood.

I challenge that myth for several reasons. Let's look at what is meant by 'good' and 'bad' neighbourhoods. Let's use as an example an upper-middle-class family living in a suburban neighbourhood in Orange County, California. We could easily substitute Tunbridge Wells near London or an Eastern suburb in Melbourne.

Our exemplary Nice Neighbourhood is populated with rather well-to-do, upper-income families headed by hard-working fathers and mothers. They are pleasure-oriented, materialistic and in debt. One or both parents have most likely been divorced and remarried. The family does not attend church, and their teenagers have experimented with drugs and alcohol.

The teens in the family are into heavy rock music, and the fifteen-year-old daughter has already had her first sexual experience. And don't forget the 'telly' as my British friends call it. The TV is on three-and-a-half hours a day. Meanwhile, the father gives his children three minutes of eye contact a day.

This 'average family' faces tremendous pressure to compromise any biblical standards of morality that has survived their spiritual isolation. The Nice Neighbourhood they live in is filled with the kind of evil that is most dangerous: that which is unseen. They face pressures and temptations to bow before the gods of materialism and pleasure daily. Their friends have more than they do, and they are racing madly to keep up. They live for themselves, and though they may be Nice people living in Nice Neighbourhood, they are separated from Christ and are part of a culture that not only condones their lifestyle, it deifies it.

The Bible speaks clearly about idolatry. God does not see this as a nice neighbourhood; this is a dangerous neighbourhood. There are various forms of evil, some overt and some more subtle. The families that live in Nice Neighbourhood have it all the more difficult because the evil that surrounds looks so good.

I challenge the myth of the good and bad neighbourhoods because I do not agree with its basic presuppositions. For most people 'good' and 'bad' are defined by safety and comfort. Further, a good neighbourhood is one that makes one comfortable because there are no 'problems' or physical challenges. All the people are 'clean' and 'neat'.

These are not biblical standards of judging good and bad neighbourhoods. Deciding where we live and how we see people should be based on different values from the rest of society. The kingdom of God is not food and drink. In fact, neighbourhoods and cities are judged in the Bible by their disobedience or obedience to God. We ought to do the same. And the place where we decide to live should be determined by God's call in our lives to be servants.

Living by biblical standards will create a spiritual momentum for our family that will keep us on our toes spiritually. It will put us on the offensive in our relationship with God, making it imperative that we spend time in prayer and spiritual warfare as a family. Our children will have a heritage of compassion, justice and evangelism. We will pass on biblical values to our children that are forged in the furnace of Christian service. What better gift could we give to them?

I live on the edge of the red light district of Amsterdam. It is a section of the city that is about ten blocks long and five blocks wide. Here the dangers are certainly not hidden. Thousands of prostitutes ply their wares on the streets and sit behind picture windows in small rooms along the canals. There are porn shops and sex clubs everywhere. Many people have AIDS. There are hundreds of hard drug users. If you walk down the wrong alley at the wrong time of day, you will be relieved of your wallet and pocket change in short order.

We first moved to the city of Amsterdam in 1973, and in 1980, when our children were five and seven years old, we moved into the red light district. We do not live here because we must, but because it is a privilege. We made the choice with our kids prayerfully, and have reviewed it with them regularly through the years. None of us have any regrets. We all love the city and celebrate its life daily. The Lord has enabled us by his grace to fulfil his calling with joy. We faced the myth that the city is not a 'nice' place to live as a family and found it held no power or validity.

## Myth Number Five: The city cannot be changed

To dissect this myth we must examine the problem of power and how it affects people. Some people have power in the city, many don't. Powerlessness means other people control your life. For those who do not have power, the affects can be devastating. Most Western Christians have no idea what powerlessness means. They have never experienced it, and have not dared to enter the world of those who do. The closest a person of means ever comes to this agonising state is to be audited by the tax authorities or accused unjustly of a crime they did not commit. Even then they can fight back, because they have the means, and the contacts, to do so. They have the will because they have dignity and resources. When one loses those things, all is lost.

### *The city personifies power*

Cities become the power centres in a modern world of communication, information, finance and government. But for most people, this means manipulation and injustice. For the Black person living in a section of the city that banks have decided to 'red zone' (where the risks are considered too great to grant personal or small business loans), a loan under normal circumstances is impossible.

Harvie Conn calls this the 'urban tower power' syndrome and traces its roots back to the tower of Babel. Though God planned for man to live in city-communities for his purposes, men rebelled and turned the city into a place to make their own name great. Cities have been spiritual-battlefields ever since for those who stand against the lordship of Christ. Evil men and women have sought to turn cities into power centres of greed, corruption and power.

The prophets called those who failed to fulfil God's purpose in the city to account for their betrayal of God's glory (Isaiah 47, Jeremiah 50, Habbakuk 1, Amos 1–3). The writer of the book of Revelation warns of impending doom to Babylon the great for her harlotries, 'Alas! alas! thou great city, thou mighty city, Babylon!' (Revelation 18:10, 16, 19).

Like a battlefield after war, the cities of our world often look like war zones. There is physical destruction and spiritual despair. Decades of welfare programmes have not turned the tide, nor has the recent bent towards conservative economic policies. Because cities have a spiritual dimension, they will only be changed by those who perceive the spiritual nature of the battle for our cities and exercise true spiritual authority.

This does not mean social programmes and standing for justice in the city is not important. Quite the contrary, cities will not be changed without those who are willing to lay down their lives for people in need. But at the heart of the matter lies a spiritual battle, and godly men and women are needed who will fight this battle.

*Urban power encounters*

If Christians are to take seriously the call to overcome evil in the city, there must be changes in the following four areas:

**(1)** We must approach the city with *faith* that God can change the urban power structures. God's sovereign power is great enough to change the most wicked city. When I first moved to the city of Amsterdam, I was overwhelmed by the vast numbers of unchurched people, and by unbelievable immorality. One Salvation Army worker told me there were sixteen thousand prostitutes working in the red-light district. Less than two per cent of greater Amsterdam's population of over one-and-a-half million people attended church. I found out that the city is the single largest supplier of child pornography to the United States, shipping over one billion dollars a year of kiddie-porn through its postal system.

It was when I started meditating on the book of Jonah that my unbelief was challenged. I recognised that I had become more impressed with the power of evil in the city than I was with God's power to change the city. God used a rebellious prophet to bring 'that great city' (Jonah 4:11) to its knees. I decided that if God could do it for Nineveh, he can do it again. Those who wield power do respond to God's grace. Harvie Conn points to other examples of change:

> A fifty-five-year reign—a trail of power highlighted by pride, child sacrifice, and syncretistic animism—ended with repentant Manasseh restored (2 Chronicles 33:1–13). Nebuchadnezzar, who boasted of 'Babylon the great' built by his own hand for the glory of his majesty (Daniel 4:30), turned from self-praise to 'exalt and honor the King of heaven' (Daniel 4:37). Ephesus, the most important city in the Roman province of Asia, was shaken by a movement to Christ among the religious power brokers.... The powerful in the world of animism discarded the secret names with secret authority in order to magnify another power name, the Lord Jesus (Acts 19:17). (Conn, p. 167.)

**(2)** There must be *repentance* for our urban prejudices and willingness to do anything God asks of us to serve in the city. White Christians have abandoned cities *en masse*. The root of the problem is one of selfishness and pride. When we truly understand the devastation that this abandonment has brought, then it will produce repentance for those who are serious about serving God.

Turning our back on neighbourhoods because of their ethnic and economic constituency is a deeply ingrained pattern that goes back to the last century. Patterns have been established in our society that are taken for granted but are rooted in prejudice and fear.

The reaction was set in motion when we fled from neighbourhoods being 'invaded' by Greeks in Australia, Irish and Blacks in the United States, and Pakistanis and West Indians in the UK. Whole subcultures and suburbs were born out of this flight-pattern. For those who were too poor to run, they stayed and fought it out, contesting control for their neighbourhoods in political power struggles.

Where was the gospel in all this? This is precisely the question that must be faced. Instead of seeing God's hand in answering our missionary prayers and bringing the people of the world to our doorstep, we reacted in anger over the supposed violation of our rights to live in neighbourhoods that we did not want invaded by outsiders. Christians did not shape how society responded to this phenomenon, but followed the lead of the ungodly.

It is time to turn the tide, but it will not happen without repentance for putting greater value on our so-called freedom to live in a 'nice neighbourhood' instead of the kingdom value of living where we are most needed.

**(3)** It is time to *return* to the city. We must return,

not as developers to change the city into our image and make a nice profit as we do so, but as servants to enable others by our presence and through our resources to rise above those things that make them powerless.

I hesitate to call for a massive move back to neighbourhoods that face challenges that many of us are not prepared to cope with. Cambodian, Pakistani, Hispanic and Samoan suburbs are not crying out for white do-gooders to invade them. But servants, learners, friends—these are needed and welcomed.

We all want genuine friends that have time to listen, who will care enough to understand and respond in a sensitive manner. In most situations this will mean a cross-cultural experience. We will be confronted with different value systems, different thinking processes, different ways of viewing time and its importance. Our whole framework for evaluating the meaning of our life will be shaken. If you are prepared for that kind of experience and willing to learn and grow through the encounter, then you are a willing candidate for God's call to the city.

**(4)** Real authority does not come from ruling over someone, but from *serving* beside them as a friend. We are quick to pronounce what other people's problems are, then impose our own solutions. This does not empower the poor, but enslaves them to one more set of dependent relationships.

Power comes when we give it away to others. Our respect for the poorest of the poor, our belief that they have much to teach us, our acknowledgement that we do not understand the problems they face and the solutions they need, are the first steps in bringing dignity to those who have been patronised and used. The ultimate test of our intentions comes when those we serve use the alternatives and resources we help create for them to turn against us. Our faith in Jesus Christ will be rejected by some of those we serve. And not only will they reject him, but some of them will turn against us as well.

Jesus faced this dilemma, and chose to embrace the ultimate rejection of those he came to save. He forgave them, endured the cross, and overcame their rejection through obedience to his Father. His example is ours. He gave up his rights, his power, but in doing so was granted a new level of spiritual authority. Many have been made righteous because of his obedience.

May God grant us the grace to lay down our lives for others, just as he did for us.

# PART 3

# THE CHURCH IN THE CITY

# CHAPTER 6

# *Incarnational Presence*

She arrived in Paris in 1881 at the age of 21. She was accompanied by two teenage friends, and they set out to turn the city on its ear. They could not have arrived at a more turbulent time: crime, disease, alcoholism and violent anti-clericalism were rampant. It was a veritable Sodom. It was the early days of the Third Republic and bitter memories of the commune still lingered on.

One of the first things Catherine Booth and her fearless band learned to do was to *pin* on their bonnet strings rather than sewing them on. This was more practical, considering that when they went into the bars and cafés to preach, men would grab their bonnet strings from behind and try to strangle them.

Obviously, the Parisians were not receptive to the gospel! Huge cobblestones were hurled into the girls' meetings, and they suffered physical and verbal abuse. By the fifth anniversary of the Salvation Army in Paris, 200 of its soldiers had been injured, 175 arrested, and one killed.

Young Catherine Booth never flinched. She had given her first sermon at the age of fourteen, and when asked about her favourite passage of the Bible, she shared her love for the story of Christ's death. When she arrived in Paris, she was dubbed 'la Capitaine'. Within eight months, and for the rest of her life, she was 'la Maréchale', the Field Marshall.

She was resented by Frenchmen for her clothes, her accent, and her optimism, but in the end they came to respect and love her dearly. She was paid the highest compliment given by the French: 'She loves France,' they said (International Herald Tribune, August 15, 1981).

Even when they fought her they admired her bold style and courage. From the beginning she refused to use an interpreter: 'If I begin with crutches I shall always need crutches.' It was said that she developed her own idiosyncratic French, translated literally from English. One hundred years after she arrived in France she was still remembered. Articles, books and special celebrations marked the anniversary of the coming of la Maréchale.

Why was she loved so dearly? Certainly the impact her preaching had on Parisian society was not small, with thousands coming to Christ through her ministry. Just as important was the depth of her care for the poor. She showed love and respect for every person she met. But above all else was her desire to become French to the French. She won their hearts by becoming one of them.

## Fleshing out the gospel

Young Kate Booth followed the example of her Lord by being among the people. She understood that at the heart of the gospel was the fact that Jesus came—

he actually lived among the very people he created. By immersing themselves in French culture and by loving the French people with total commitment, Catherine Booth and her team created an incarnational presence. They not only declared the gospel with their words, they demonstrated it with their lives.

In John 1:14 it says of Jesus, 'And the Word became flesh and dwelt among us, full of grace and truth; we have beheld his glory....' Further, Jesus says to his disciples towards the end of his earthly ministry, 'As the Father sent me, even so I send you' (20:21). Jesus was concerned that the disciples go into all the world in the same manner in which he came—in humility, living among the people as one of them.

God did not send his son in a fiery chariot, riding above the masses, shouting messages of prophetic warning. Jesus was one with people. He was born in simplicity and raised in obscurity. His mother's reputation was questionable, and his father died when he was a youth. He spoke the language of the common man, and learned a trade.

God did not remain aloof from our problems, but entered into them by becoming a man and living a normal life. His authority is rooted not only in who he is, but also in the fact that the Creator stepped into his creation.

The coming of the Lord Jesus Christ as servant of man and Son of God is not only God's way of reconciling his creation to himself, it is also a demonstration of how we should act in a fallen world. It is not only the means by which God offers salvation to the world, it is the model for the church to follow as it lives and serves in the city.

## The church in the city

Christian presence that is divorced from the example of the Lord Jesus is not Christian. No matter what is said by our words, if we do not follow the example of his servanthood our lives deny the truth of what we say. Truth is lived and spoken. Authority to speak into people's lives is derived from our commitment to live among them as servants.

This is why television and radio evangelism ministries can quickly undermine their own calling. Those who minister through these mediums can create an impression of personalness that is impossible to live out. When a person says that 'it is good to be with you today in your living room' or 'I am praying just for you right now' they are not only speaking a lie but shortcutting the way God has instructed us to serve those who are in need.

This does not mean that we cannot use these mediums to communicate the gospel, but it does mean that our responsibility to do so ethically is under greater pressure. There is no substitute for the presence of the local church, demonstrating the gospel by living, working and rubbing shoulders with sceptical pagans. Our corporate presence as the body of Christ is just that—we are the body of Christ. Not in a mystical sense, nor are we deity, but God has chosen to reveal himself through the church. In the Old Testament he dwelt in a special way in a tabernacle. When Christ came he dwelt in a human body. Now the whole church is his body, the meeting place between God and man.

When the church fails to *be* the gospel, our witness is no longer viable. But when we are all that God intended us to be, the local church becomes a powerful witness to Christ. What are we intended to be as the body of Christ on the earth? We learn the answer to that question by discovering how Jesus incarnated himself on the earth.

## Leaving and letting go

The incarnation involved several stages. The first is that Jesus left his home. He let go of his rights in heaven: the glory, the closeness to his father, the power and privilege of who he was. If we are to follow his example, it will also mean letting go of our home, our culture, our family and friends, and all that is precious and important to us. It says in Philippians 2:6, 'though he was in the form of God, he did not count equality with God a thing to be grasped.' Leaving means there is something to be left behind. We let go of people and things that are important to us because of a higher calling. We no longer grasp hold of what is ours, but lay it down to follow Jesus and to serve others.

It is possible to be a Christian and not be an incarnational Christian. It is also possible to commit ourselves to follow Christ and yet never truly live among people as one who is called to serve. We can start the journey without completing it. The incarnational model of the Lord Jesus compels us not only to accept Christ as our Saviour, it demands that we leave behind our cultural baggage, our rights and our attachments to citizenship in earthly kingdoms.

## Going

The incarnation also meant 'going'. Leaving heaven would not have meant much for Jesus if he had not completed the journey and come to earth. He adopted a new home. He spoke another language. He lived among a people he had not known in the same manner before. He not only let go of his privileges and rights in theory, but in reality. He was not just willing to do what he did, he actually did it.

This truth does not just apply to missionaries. This is at the heart of the Christian life for all believers. Every major decision we make in life as individuals and as congregations should be made in the light of the incarnation. When we are offered better jobs, do we ask ourselves if it will help us be more like Jesus, help serve his purposes on earth, or do we assume that if there is more pay involved, God is blessing us and therefore it is automatically his will to accept the new position? Are we more concerned about being upwardly mobile than serving those in need around us? Are we bent on getting ahead or getting where God is sending us? The two directions need not be incompatible but often are.

## Living amongst

Jesus' great journey culminated in his birth as the child of Joseph and Mary. He became flesh and *dwelt* among us. For thirty years he lived as one of us. He was the Son of God, but he emptied himself of his divine prerogatives and lived the simple lifestyle of a Palestinian boy. He played their games, spoke their language, grieved at their funerals and rejoiced at their weddings. In doing so, he experienced all the pains of our common humanity. He voluntarily entered into the ordinariness of our lives.

Therefore, it can be said of him, 'We have not a high priest who is unable to sympathise with our weaknesses, but one who in every respect has been tempted as we are, yet without sin' (Hebrews 4:15). He understands us, not just because he is infinite in knowledge, but because he has lived with us and among us. He has experienced our joys and our sorrows, felt our passions, faced our temptations and carried our spiritual burdens.

And he did this for joy. He anticipated and experienced the pleasure there is, not only in pleasing his father in heaven, but in serving others. He was not introducing a form of spiritual masochism by giving up all that was his in heaven. He willingly laid down what was rightfully his out of his great love for us.

Ultimately he lived among us so that we would know reality. He endured the shame and pain of the cross, he went through the misunderstandings, he experienced the mundaneness of our lives and waited patiently thirty-three years and then offered himself as he did, so that we would be reconciled to the Father.

And he has called us to do the same. To follow his example, believers will embrace the challenge to get involved in people's lives. Building relationships with those who do not know Christ will be our consuming passion and will take precedence over seeking pleasure for ourselves.

## Listening and caring

You might say that Jesus spent thirty years listening and three years speaking. Or as one Japanese evangelist put it, 'We have twice as many ears as mouths, so we should spend twice as much time listening as we do talking.'

*He did not just hear words, but hearts.* He really listened. He stopped at the well at noontime to converse with a Samaritan woman. He went out of his way to be with people. This kind of listening takes time. It means inconvenience and interruption. It means feeling what others feel and weeping when they weep, not so we can win them to our cause but because we genuinely care.

*Listening means understanding.* No one likes to be patronised or talked down to. We want to know that we are understood and respected. Without it we won't feel secure in opening up our hearts to someone.

*Listening means acceptance.* Not that we want someone to agree with us all the time, but we appreciate it when a person has the ability to see our failures and to love us unconditionally. Deep inside we all know that acceptance does not mean agreement, but that a person is committed to us no matter how badly we blow it.

*Listening means respect.* We dignify the lives of others by taking seriously the expression of their likes and dislikes, their dreams and doubts, their joys and sorrows. Every person is created in the image of God, and therefore has great worth. Every aspiration they have, every decision they make has great value, whether or not it is consistent with the Christian faith. When we allow a person's status in life—their poverty or their wealth, their political or moral views—to block our respect for their basic humanity, we have communicated to them by our attitude that we do not take them seriously, we do not respect them.

Jesus was able to transcend the fallenness of those he lived with and show them he cared for them as people. In spite of his awesome holiness and infinite power, Jesus demonstrated his commitment to listen and care for Samaritans and women, prostitutes and tax collectors, children and indeed anyone whom society counted as of little worth; they were of great importance to him. This is what the incarnation was all about.

Unfortunately, many Christians have not demonstrated this same willingness or ability. By our attitudes toward non-Christians we actually communicate just the opposite of what our Lord did. Many evangelicals have allowed Christianity to become a religion, something more important than loving people. They make doctrine more important than being like Jesus, and substitute trust in creeds and confessions for their trust in Christ. They are in danger of creating a Christianity in their own image and falling down and worshipping themselves.

## Dying

In his death Jesus laid down his rights. He deserved respect, acceptance and honour. He was the Saviour of mankind, the Lamb of God, Messiah, the Word of God, Creator of the universe, the beginning and the end. But rather than demand what was rightfully his, he willingly gave up his rights.

Instead he chose to become a servant. He accepted slander and abuse, bitterness and rejection, because he chose another way. He chose the way of the cross because it was the way to men's hearts. He did not want a kingdom of slaves who served him because they had to, but an army of love-slaves whose loyalty was won by the love of their master.

It was for this reason that he performed mighty deeds; he was intent on loving people into the kingdom. He was moved with compassion by the needs of his creation and responded out of his great love to heal them. It was not sympathy that motivated him, nor was it a fascination with his divine power. He had no need to prove he was a man of great faith. He simply loved people.

It was this love that sent Jesus into the world: 'For God so loved the world....' (John 3:16). And it is the same love that will thrust us into the world. When his love fills our hearts it will compel us to lay down our lives, to give up our rights, and to serve others, even till death if necessary.

Jesus said to his disciples, 'As the Father has sent me, even so I send you' (John 20:21). This commission is ours; it is not for a small group of men who lived long ago. The world is our home. *We* are the sent ones.

The incarnation is our example, our model for life and for mission. And as God's people it is our guiding light for the city. Not only is the city created and loved by God, it is a key place of calling and service as local congregations. For those who grasp the goodness of God in allowing them this privilege, the city is our sacred place, the place of our opportunity to follow the example of our Lord.

For those congregations who embrace the example of the Lord Jesus as their model for corporate church life, the city will more often than not be the place to go to, our home while sojourning without a lasting home. It is the place to live out the gospel as servants, laying down our lives so that others may find life.

# CHAPTER 7

# *Apostles to the City*

The young couple sitting before me poured out their hearts. They were incensed by the idolatry they saw around them. They explained they had a definite missionary calling to the nation of India. But when they arrived, they were shocked at the vast number of idols that people worshipped in this strange and fascinating land.

They had read about Hinduism, but when they saw it being lived out before their eyes, when they visited the Hindu temples, saw the monkey gods and experienced Indian people actually bowing before graven images, it made them angry.

They explained their plan. They wanted to go on the streets, to the temples, visit the homes of Hindu priests, and explain what the Bible said about idolatry. They felt they should warn the people of God's judgement to come.

This all sounded very well. But something was missing. I asked them three simple questions: 'I understand how important it is for us to speak about idolatry from a biblical perspective, but before you do that let me ask you some questions. First, can you assure me that you have some Indian friends who are non-Christians that you know by name, that have been in your home and you in theirs, and whom you like as people?'

The couple sat with a puzzled looked for a time. The silence that ensued became embarrassing as they racked their brains trying to remember the name of someone they remembered meeting on a street corner and having a cup of tea with. 'No, not really, but we plan to do that. We've only been here eight months....'

Next question: 'Well then, can you tell me three or four things about this culture that you deeply appreciate and have come to respect?'

Again a puzzled look, the eyebrows raised and the forehead furrowed in deep thought. 'Why no, of course not. Can't you see, this country is ruled by demon spirits. It's totally demonic, everything about the country has been destroyed by Hinduism. Can't you see that?'

I went on to the third question: 'You have been here eight months, you've had enough time to experience the culture, to meet people, to see the needs of this land. Have you fasted for India, have you lost sleep because of the burden of prayer on your hearts for this land? Have you wept for India?'

The silence this time was indeed embarrassing. The realisation began to dawn on this angry young couple of the importance of my questions. They didn't respect the culture or believe there was anything good in it. They knew no Indians by name nor had any Indian friends. And they had not wept over the land.

With great sadness in my heart I explained that

they had no authority to preach the gospel in India. Until they saw the good in the culture, until they knew Indian friends personally and were having social and friendship needs met through their personal interrelationships with non-Christians, and until they were broken-hearted with a deep love for the people, they would never have the right to preach the gospel to Indians or lift their finger in even a gentle rebuke about the idolatry of the land.

## Seeing through God's eyes

Authority to preach the gospel and minister in the name of Jesus Christ in a city or nation is gained not just by being called by God, but by fulfilling the conditions of that call.

When I came to the city of Amsterdam I spent six months simply walking the streets of every major neighbourhood in the city. I rode trams and metros and buses, getting a feel for the city. I asked God to let me see the city through his eyes. I asked him to help me understand her culture. I read every book I could get my hands on about Amsterdam. I would sit in the coffee shops and the 'Brown cafés', listening to the people. I developed a fondness for the openhearted, humour-loving, sea-faring Amsterdamer.

It was out of those many months of walking her streets that I grew to love the city of Amsterdam. In fact, now I not only love it, I like it! I am an Amsterdamer.

There is a perception that the Bible is an anti-urban book. People seek justification for their urban-racism: 'David, after all, was a shepherd.' This prejudice is not rooted in God's heart, and the Bible makes that abundantly clear. There are over 1,400 references to cities in the Bible, many expressing

God's love and concern for the people of the city and the citizens surrounding it.

There are many examples that flesh out this reality. I have chosen four men and four cities to examine in a closer way.

## An unknown layman and the city of firsts

Antioch was the first city to have a Gentile congregation. It was the first city where the church sent out missionaries. It was the first church that sent financial relief to another church, and it was the first city in which the followers of Christ had the wonderful distinction of being called 'Christians'.

This magnificent city was located on the Orontes river, and was the capital of the Roman province of Syria—the third most important city in the Roman Empire. It was a multi-racial, militaristic, idolatrous, wealthy, sex-mad city. In one word, it was a 'modern' city.

Interestingly, the church at Antioch had some of the most colourful experiences recorded in the Bible. It was in Antioch that Paul confronted Peter face to face, and it was here that the controversy over circumcision arose.

According to Charles Ludwig in his book *Cities in New Testament Times* (Accent Books), the site for the founding of Antioch was selected by Alexander the Great. After he had defeated the Persian king, Darius III, Alexander marched south where he began a seven-month-long siege of the city of Tyre. He stopped just east of the city, where he drank from a spring. The water was so sweet and refreshing that he decided to build a city on the spot.

Eventually, Seleucus—one of Alexander's generals—

became the ruler of Syria. Burning with a passion to perpetuate the name of his father Antiochus, Seleucus founded and named the ... city after him.' (*Cities in New Testament Times,* page 78.)

The church in Antioch became a great spiritual powerhouse. Many have modelled their church life after the church in Antioch. Although the church was led by such great men as Paul and Barnabas, it was actually started by an unknown layman fleeing persecution in the city of Jerusalem. Acts 11:19–21 says:

> Now those who were scattered because of the persecution that arose over Stephen travelled as far as Phoenicia and Cyprus and Antioch, speaking the word to none except Jews. But there were some of them, men of Cyprus and Cyrene, who on coming to Antioch spoke to the Greeks also, preaching the Lord Jesus. And the hand of the Lord was with them, and a great number that believed turned to the Lord.

When news of the growth of the church reached Jerusalem, they sent Barnabas to Antioch. He saw the grace of the Lord upon the church and rejoiced with them. Under Barnabas' leadership a large company was added to the church. Barnabas went to Tarsus to look for Paul and brought him back with him to Antioch to help lead the blossoming work of God in the city.

Many have wondered at the strength and the impact the church had upon the city of Antioch. What was the secret of its growth and its spiritual power? There are a number of things that stand out about this wonderful church which we can learn for church life in the city.

*The power of fellowship.* The church in Antioch was a multiracial fellowship made up of Africans,

Europeans and Asians. Both Jew and Gentile worshipped together in harmony.

If the church today is to make an impact upon the cities of our modern world, we too must break across the racial barriers and the cultural dividers in society. The church has to demonstrate that it has the power to bring all classes together. Although the church may grow more quickly along cultural and ethnic lines, we must never allow these lines to become walls. If we want power, there must be unity and that unity must be a demonstration that that which divides society will never divide the church.

*The power of team leadership.* When Barnabas brought Saul to Antioch he initiated a God-designed plan for leadership in the church. Barnabas realised that he could not lead the church alone, he needed help. Eventually that leadership team grew to include prophets, teachers, evangelists and apostles as well as pastors. It was a well-rounded group whose gifts complemented one another.

This kind of plurality always needs a 'senior among equals'. Equality does not mean that we do not recognise those with senior maturity or anointing. Nor does it mean that we do not recognise a need for orderly authority in our midst. If we are to have a wise and stable fellowship, we need to have a team of men and women with varieties of gifts and personalities that hold one another accountable and provide balance and direction to the body they serve.

*The power of every-member ministry.* When we read about the church in Antioch we read about a church that encourages members to be involved in the ministry. The leaders were seen as equippers, the people as the ministers. It was a layman who started the church and it was ordinary people by their witness in the shops and in the market places that earned the authority for the believers to be known as the followers of Christ, 'Christians'.

*The power of teaching.* Acts 13:1 says that there were 'prophets and teachers, Barnabas, Symeon....' We can never underestimate the power of teaching God's word. The authoritative proclamation of the eternal truths of Scripture make a powerful impact on the lives of people. The result is that the church grows in spiritual maturity and in number. The church in Antioch was taught the ways of God. New Christians were taught how to be faithful to their master, and leaders were taught how to equip the saints and minister faithfully to the people of God.

*The power of worship and prayer.* It is a fascinating insight into early church life to see the leadership team in the church of Antioch meeting together for a time of fasting and worship (Acts 13:1–3). It was during this time when the Holy Spirit spoke to them that they were to set aside Barnabas and Paul for missionary work.

This points to the fact that this was not a static form of worship that was controlled by pre-set liturgy with no opportunity for the Holy Spirit to speak to his people. In some way that we do not understand, but most likely included prophetic utterances, they were able to hear from the Lord and his response to their petitions. This is further made clear by the fact that recognised prophets were allowed to foretell by the Spirit that there would be a famine at some point in the future (Acts 11:28).

If the church of Jesus Christ is to be all that it is intended to be, we must encourage the function of spiritual gifts that create an expectancy in the hearts of the people that God will respond to them and speak specifically to their questions and needs.

The church in the city must be a worshipping

church. Celebration is a vital witness to the world, and it also enables the people to be refreshed spiritually in the presence of the Lord.

Joy is a vital ingredient of the life of the church in the city. To quench this joy through heavy-handed leadership and staid worship styles not only discourages urban church growth, it also stunts the maturing of God's people.

*The power of a missionary vision.* It is obvious that the church in Antioch was concerned about others. This is evidenced in their involvement with the poor (Acts 11:29), and their willingness to send out the very best of their leadership in missionary endeavours.

The test of any church's commitment to mission is its willingness to send its very best to help in the missionary enterprise. Far too many urban churches become overwhelmed with the needs around them and lose their world vision. A church that becomes ingrown and insular will discourage big-hearted people with potential for Christian service from attending the church. They will soon learn that there is a grasping, controlling spirit rather than a generous spirit among the leaders. They will discover that the church leadership is not committed to building up their gifts and sending them out, but rather keeping them there to build up the local church programme.

One pastor I know believes he is to discourage all interest in mission on the part of individual lay people in the congregation. His philosophy is that if God wants them to go, they will overcome his wet-blanket approach and make it somehow. The lack of Christlikeness and generosity in this attitude has discouraged many in his congregation from following Christ in Christian service. Though this church has been blessed by God, I have often wondered how much more blessing it would have experienced had the pastor had a more Christlike approach to the longings of some of his parishioners to be involved in mission.

The pastor and ministry team that decides to equip God's people for service will reap the reward of seeing those they serve extend the outreach of the church throughout the world.

*The power of Christlikeness.* In Antioch the believers were first called Christians. Something about the lives of the people warranted a response from the non-Christian community. In that centre of idolatry and commercial competition, the Christians made such an impact on the city that they had to be recognised.

The power of the witness of the church in Antioch is an encouragement that we too can make an impact upon the cities of our world. The price we must pay for this influence is that we live our lives exactly like our Lord Jesus.

## Nineveh and the proud prophet

After walking the streets of Amsterdam for six months I was overwhelmed. I passed block after block of tenement houses. I walked through high-rise apartment complexes with buildings that were hundreds of yards long and housed up to 1,500 people per building. I saw council estates that were poverty-stricken, neighbourhoods that were run down. I passed hundreds of thousands of people who did not know Jesus Christ. My research had shown me that there were eight or nine churches that were evangelical in the city of Amsterdam. Church attendance was less than 2%; I was told that one tenth of 1% of the population in the city were committed Christians, though of course no one could really say for sure.

I learned that Amsterdam exported more child pornography to the United States than any other single city in the world, almost one billion dollars a year. I learned that it was the sex capital of Europe, and that forty to fifty thousand homosexuals visited Amsterdam every weekend. I saw with my own eyes the sex clubs and the child pornography. I saw hawkers standing in front of theatres calling people to watch live sex acts. I saw advertisements in magazines placed by city officials proudly proclaiming the pleasure of Amsterdam's 'world-renowned red light district'. I saw hundreds of teenage prostitutes on the streets of Amsterdam; I was told that there were 16,000 prostitutes in the call services and sitting behind the windows in the red light district. I knew that there were at least 10,000 drug addicts and that heroin and cocaine were sold openly on many street corners.

I experienced a city with a restive political atmosphere and a leftist youth movement that was deeply concerned about world problems, such as apartheid and nuclear armament. I visited 'kraak houses' which young people had illegally broken into and turned into their squat-houses. I heard the passion of these young people as they spoke of economic injustice and the unfairness of rich landlords holding onto their empty buildings to push up rental prices in the free sector of the economy.

I saw no hope for the city of Amsterdam. Until I read the book of Jonah.

It was in this little prophetic book that I discovered that God used a proud prophet to turn around one of the most wicked cities in the history of mankind. Nineveh had reigned for 1,500 years as a ruthless city-state without being defeated by another military power. The walls around Nineveh were wide enough to drive three cars side by side. Traces of at least two walls around the city have been found and some archaeologists estimate there were up to eleven different walls surrounding the city.

We know from reading the book of Jonah that it took three days to walk across the city (Jonah 3). Nineveh was famous for its military power and cruelty to its foes. It took 11,000 slaves ten years to build the king's palace. Its temples were famous for prostitution.

Nineveh was the capital of Syria, Israel's arch-enemies to the north. They often invaded villages on the northern border of Israel and thus were hated by the people of God. It is no wonder that Jonah resisted the call of God to go and proclaim not only the Lord's judgement, but also his salvation to the people of Nineveh. Jonah was afraid that the Lord would bless his enemies: 'I pray thee, Lord, is not this what I said when I was yet in my country? That is why I made haste to flee to Tarshish; for I knew that thou art a gracious God and merciful, slow to anger, and abounding in steadfast love, and repentest of evil' (Jonah 4:2).

We learn certain vital lessons from this book that apply to the church, no matter if we live in a great city, suburb or small town. If ever there was a picture of the church in today's world, it is painted for us in the opening verses of this little book. God speaks to the prophet and calls him to go to the city. The prophet is alarmed and runs the other way. He goes to the port, buys a ticket and heads for Tarshish. While on the boat a great storm arises, and Jonah sleeps while Nineveh goes to hell.

*We learn in this book that God loves cities.* He not only loved the Nineveh that he called Jonah to, but he loves the Ninevehs of our world. He loves Liverpool and London, he loves Sydney and Melbourne, he loves Auckland, and he loves Washington DC. The question we must ask is this: do we love cities the way God does? Are we more like Jonah and his reaction to the city of Nineveh, or are we like the Lord in his commitment to love people?

*We learn in this book that certain cities are strategic in God's purposes.* God focused his attention on the city of Nineveh not only because it was a source of great evil influence, but because it was also to be a source of great blessing. He chose Nineveh because he wanted to make it an example of righteousness. A revival broke out in Nineveh that swept the entire city, from the king to the most common labourer. What an impact this must have had on the villages around it. And yet, it seems the revival was cut short because of Jonah's reaction. What would have happened if the prophet had responded differently?

*We learn in this book that God uses weak human beings.* When I first read the book of Jonah I was encouraged. I thought to myself, 'If God can use Jonah, he can use me!' Have you thought, 'God can't use me, I don't have theological training' or 'I can't do it, I'm not as gifted as this person or that person'?

It is the weak people of the world that confound the mighty. It is the very fact that we know we cannot do something which gives us our greatest qualification—if we call upon the Lord. Do not be more impressed with the evil of the city than with the greatness of God. His greatness through you can make a mighty difference.

*We learn in this book that God uses the simplicity of preaching.* What a powerful lesson, and yet it is so often overlooked by the church. At the very heart of all mission work, at the heart of all concern for poor, must be the proclamation of the good news of Jesus

Christ, whether it is done through drama, music, medical work, community development, or church planting. Everything we do must be centred around Christ.

*We learn there is hope for cities.* In his book *The Meaning of the City*, Jacques Ellul reaches the conclusion that cities are held under the sway of principalities and powers. Pessimism comes through in Ellul's book, particularly in the contrast he draws between the city of God and the city of man. Though Ellul's point is well taken, that humankind seeks to create a false, alternative community in the city as a result of their rebellion against God, we must not forget that it was God who put the longing for community for city and togetherness in man's heart in the beginning.

Going further than Ellul, many sociologists are overwhelmed by the problems of fallen mankind when brought to focus in the city. But rather than join in this pessimism, it is important to remember that God ordained the city, and that when man lives by God's precepts the city will be redeemed: 'When it goes well with the righteous, the city rejoices (Proverbs 11:10).

Further, the revival and redemption of a city like Nineveh encourages us that no city is beyond God's redemption.

It is further a warning to all those who bear the name of Christ that God intends to be at work in the city whether we co-operate with him or not. His sovereign will shall be done. Men and women will seek him and find him. He will redeem peoples in neighbourhoods and cities. The question is, will we be on the outside of what God is doing, looking on, or will we be in the flow of God's redemptive acts in the city?

## Paul and Philippi

It is difficult to select one city that represents the amazing contribution the apostle Paul made to the expansion of the church in the first century. Paul was an urban apostle. Athens, Rome, Corinth, Jerusalem, Antioch, Ephesus and many other cities felt the impact of the ministry of this great man. But one city's significance outshines them all, and that was the first city to receive the gospel in Europe. The Holy Spirit had forbade Paul and his team to go into Asia, and instead gave a compelling vision that they were to preach the gospel in Macedonia. Ten miles along from the tiny port city of Neapolis lay the ancient city of Philippi. It was named in honour of Philip II of Macedon, the one-eyed father of Alexander the Great.

In 334 BC, using Philippi as one of his major European bases, Alexander the Great invaded Asia. Now, in stark contrast, Paul was using Asia as his base to invade Europe. Paul's tiny missionary band was comprised of Silas, often called Silvanus, Timothy (who joined him in Lystra and whom Paul often referred to as his beloved son), and Luke, the gentile physician who joined with Paul at Troas. Determined to preach the gospel in Asia, God arrested Paul by a dramatic vision that appeared to him in the night while he was in the city of Troas. In what today we might call a charismatic experience, Paul was brought up short by the living God, and no doubt began to ponder deeply the implication of crossing over into the continent of Europe.

As Paul sailed into Neapolis, and then trudged the ten-mile journey up to Philippi, he was no doubt aware of the history of this great city. It was here that Brutus and Cassius—assassins of Julius Caesar—

clashed with the armies of Octavian and Anthony. Being a citizen of Tarsus, Paul had a distinct reason to recall the importance of that great battle.

Charles Ludwig points out that following Caesar's assassination Cassius, who was the main mover behind the plot, with his brother-in-law Brutus, had taken flight from Rome. Cassius eventually ended up in Tarsus, ordered his soldiers to live in the homes of the wealthy, and in the words of Ludwig, 'coldly announced that he wouldn't leave until he was paid nine million dollars'. To raise that amount—in those days a fantastic sum—public lands in Tarsus were auctioned, silver and gold vessels from the temples were melted, and the free were sold into slavery. First to be enslaved were boys, then girls, then men and women, and then finally old people. Many killed themselves rather than submit. Though this had happened many years before the time of Paul, every citizen in Tarsus would have known the terrible things done by Cassius.

When Paul of Tarsus entered the city of Philippi, he must have wondered how God was going to lead him to penetrate this city. His normal pattern was to go to a synagogue and preach. Finding no synagogue in the city of Philippi, Paul was forced to adopt new and creative methods. He heard that there was a place of prayer by the riverside where a number of women gathered to worship each Sabbath. It is fascinating to note that Paul did not hesitate to proclaim the gospel to a group of women. And it is even more fascinating to note that the first church to be planted on the continent of Europe was made up of female converts and led initially by a woman. Lydia compelled Paul and his team to receive hospitality with her (Acts 16:15), and it was in her home that the church in Philippi gathered for worship and instruction.

Not only is this church significant because it illustrates Paul's openness to women in general, and specifically women in leadership, it also demonstrates the power of a church with a missionary vision. Writing to the Philippian church ten years after the church had been planted in Philippi, in AD 60, Paul thanks the Philippians for their partnership in mission. He says he prayed with joy because of their partnership in the gospel from the first day until then. (Philippians 1:4–5; 4:15–16).

Dr Bill Lane, a New Testament scholar, stresses the need to appreciate the extent of the Philippians' partnership with Paul. He pointed out, in a series of lectures given to Youth With A Mission staff in Amsterdam, that their missionary ministry was extended through Paul, their adopted missionary, to Thessalonica, which in turn spread the gospel throughout Asia. They also supported Paul and prayed for him while he was in Corinth. This enabled him to devote his full attention to the ministry of preaching the gospel while in that city.

When there was a famine in Judea, God placed a burden on Paul's heart to bring a gift to the Christians in Jerusalem. Paul talks about the participation of the Philippians in that ministry of mercy as well (2 Corinthians 8:1–5).

Paul also thanks the Philippians for their involvement with him in the city of Rome (Philippians 2:25; 4:18). The Philippian letter was primarily a thank you letter to the church, after they had sent a gift to Paul while he was under house arrest in the city of Rome. Going further than sending their finances, they sent a gifted member of the congregation, Epaphroditus, to work with Paul in the training of believers in the imperial city.

When you think of one congregation impacting

such cities as Thessalonica, Corinth, Jerusalem and Rome, you begin to understand the breadth of the vision of this church. The ministry of Paul in these cities included the training of lay leadership, caring for the poor and the needy, proclaiming the gospel, and church planting.

The church in Philippi and its commitment to missions, its willingness to adopt a missionary that was not from their own church, and the breadth and extent of their vision, is an example to churches today. This is no selfish congregation with a limited kingdom perspective. They were willing to stand with Paul through thick and thin, even when he was under arrest. They sent not only their money but they sent their best people. They participated with him in every sort of ministry including relief and development, church planting, evangelism and education and training.

Dr Lane points out that seventy-five years after Paul wrote his letter to the Philippians, Polycarp—the senior pastor of the church in Smyrna—wrote these words to the Philippians:

> I have greatly rejoiced with you in our Lord Jesus Christ ... because the strong root of your faith, which was spoken of in days long past, endures even until now and brings forth fruit to our Lord Jesus Christ (First Letter of Polycarp to the Philippians).

## Nehemiah and Jerusalem

The church's involvement in large cities must include a commitment to rebuilding the city's social, familial, educational, medical and economic support systems. This commitment to urban community development needs to include a wide range of activities that embrace everything from prophetic denunciation of injustice, musical presentations of the gospel, counsellors to care for the wounded, professional workers to help with training and the rebuilding of the community, electing godly men to roles of government to ensure that corruption is uprooted and righteousness is upheld, and evangelism and church planting.

This all-encompassing approach to community development is spelled out by Roger Greenway in his book *Apostles to the City*:

> Nehemiah, the architect of Jerusalem's urban renewal, had something very special in mind for this day ... the returned exiles from Babylon gathered at the Water Gate of the temple in Jerusalem. They were celebrating the Feast of Trumpets, a sacred festival that God had ordained as an annual celebration on the first day of the seventh month.... He had put forward every effort to inspire the people to rebuild the ruined city. They had cleared away the rubble, erected the walls, and built new houses. It had been a tremendous undertaking and Nehemiah was proud of the people's accomplishments. But something more was needed. Nehemiah realized that moral and religious reforms had to be made to give the nation a spiritual foundation that would set it apart from other nations and prevent the kind of decay that had precipitated its former destruction. For social and political reforms to take hold in a way that would please God and preserve the people, spiritual renewal must occur. This could happen only if God's word was known, understood and obeyed.' (*Apostles to the City*, page 45.)

Following are principles from the book of Nehemiah that apply specifically to community development in an urban context. It is important to note that there is an integration of practical and spiritual dimensions in the book of Nehemiah. It is at the same time a book of leadership principles, teaching on spiritual warfare, a practical guide to urban renewal, and a book that deals with justice and righteousness.

*We learn from the book of Nehemiah that urban community development should be birthed in intercession, fasting and confession of sin.* Nehemiah heard a report about the sins of the people, and in a wonderful act of identification confessed the sins of the people of Israel as his own sins, 'We have sinned against thee...' (Nehemiah 1:6). When we see the conditions of cities, it should drive us to our knees in deep sorrow and grief. Anger towards the injustice of those who have destroyed the city must affect us to the point that we identify with the selfishness that has caused the problems. Otherwise there can be no weeping and mourning as Nehemiah did.

Further, it is important to note that it was in the place of prayer that Nehemiah received inspiration and direction from the Lord on how to be involved personally in the rebuilding of Jerusalem. Action without prayer is only human enthusiasm; action born out of prayer is divine inspiration and direction.

Nehemiah used the power structures of the day for the benefit of his people. He did not set himself on a collision course with the non-Jewish king that he served, but rather he appealed for his help and co-operation in rebuilding the walls of Jerusalem.

Rather than treating governmental structures as our enemies, we should seek every way possible to find their co-operation and their goodwill (Nehemiah 2:2–3, 6). Obviously there are times when we will be on a collision course with corrupt officials and unco-operative power structures but every effort should be given to win their favour. When that does not happen, the Bible speaks to the importance of exposing and resisting unjust power structures.

*Nehemiah took time to understand the needs of Jerusalem.* Too often development work is done on the spur of the moment. Long-term development projects take over where disaster relief finishes. There is no excuse for a lack of thorough research and preparation for the projects we take on. Nehemiah inspected the walls of Jerusalem in order to know exactly what the needs were that he was going to be involved in (Nehemiah 2:11–16).

*Spiritual opposition in the form of criticism, mockery, attempted bribery, and physical threats should be expected when we are involved in urban community development* (Nehemiah 4:1–3; 5:1–6; 6:1–14). Community development is a spiritual task. Seeking to meet the physical, emotional, mental and spiritual needs of any people will bring a swift retaliation from spiritual powers that seek to destroy people's lives.

We must study God's word carefully to understand the spiritual dimension of power encounters, and understand the weapons and authority that are at our disposal as believers. The Bible makes it clear that our weapons are not carnal but spiritual. We must learn to respond in the opposite spirit to our enemies if we are to win spiritual battles.

For example:

▷ When Nehemiah was criticised by Sanballat and Tobiah his response was to pray and to keep working (Nehemiah 4:1–6).

▷ When Nehemiah was threatened with physical abuse, he responded by taking the precaution of setting armed guards to watch over their property and protect the people (Nehemiah 4:7–9).

▷ When the people became afraid, Nehemiah spent time strengthening and encouraging the people, as well as renewing the weak portions in the wall

(Nehemiah 4:13–14).

- ▷ When there was a threat because the people were separated from each other and were vulnerable to attack, Nehemiah established a communications system so that they could support one another (Nehemiah 4:19–20).
- ▷ Nehemiah took practical precautions and taught the people basic survival skills (Nehemiah 4:21–23).
- ▷ When Nehemiah learned that there was economic injustice within the community of Jewish believers, and that some of the people were exploiting others unjustly, he became angry. He exposed the corruption and brought charges against those who were involved. He held a public assembly and righted the things that had been done wrong. He personally participated in rectifying the economic situations by using his own financial resources to do all that he could to make things right. Nehemiah was not afraid to confront corruption, injustice and economic unrighteousness within the congregation of the people. This won the trust of the people and allowed them to work in peace and harmony (Nehemiah 5:6–13).
- ▷ Nehemiah lived a restrained lifestyle and so modelled before the people an example of economic frugality. This prevented him from being open to any charge from his enemies that he was exploiting the people for selfish gain (Nehemiah 5:14–15).
- ▷ When Nehemiah was lured into a trap by his enemies, he refused to be engaged in fruitless discussions with people that were opposed to the

work of God. He would not meet with Sanballat and Tobiah (Nehemiah 6:1–3).

▷ Sanballat sought to manipulate Nehemiah through attacks on his reputation. Nehemiah did not give into the demands of his enemies. He answered them truthfully by declaring the facts, but he realised that the motive of his enemies was to strike fear into his heart. He turned to God for help, recognising that the battle was the Lord's (Nehemiah 6:7–9).

▷ Nehemiah discerned when false prophets came against him to prophesy threats and warnings. He would not compromise himself in any way in response to the attacks of these false teachers and prophets (Nehemiah 6:10–14).

*Nehemiah understood the importance of teaching God's law and proclaiming God's word in urban renewal* (Nehemiah 8). He insisted on reading the word of God publicly and called the people into account for how they were living. He was not a man who ignored the spiritual dimensions of the lives of people at the price of caring for them physically. He encouraged a revival movement that was rooted in repentance and public restitution. He asked for the resumption of worship and delegated this responsibility to those who were anointed for the task (Nehemiah 9:1–8, 32–38).

*Nehemiah lived amongst the people that he was called to serve.* It is impossible to serve people meaningfully in a community development project without living among them (Nehemiah 11:1–2). Though this is impossible in some situations, e.g. western families living with urban slum dwellers in third-world cities, every effort must be made to live as close to the people as possible.

*Nehemiah had a holistic view of community development*

*that integrated worship and celebration in the urban renewal process* (Nehemiah 12:44–47). All too often people have a narrow view of community development. They think of job training, political lobbying and feeding the poor. However, worship is also to be a part of the process. Nehemiah was not afraid to encourage the people to celebrate. At one point there was so much sadness in the camp over the revelation of their sins, Nehemiah declared a love feast and asked the people to stop mourning so they might receive the grace of God (Nehemiah 8:9–12).

*Nehemiah stood against false prophets, false teachers and ungodly priests who were corrupting the city* (Nehemiah 13:1–9). Today the inner cities need a revival among those who are exploiting Black and Asian churches and using them for their own gain. False priests, whether they be white TV evangelists or black pastors with big cars, need to be confronted with their sins. The church must cleanse itself.

The work on the wall in Jerusalem was completed in fifty-two days. God blessed the work of Nehemiah's hands because he was a man of integrity and courage. His balance is an example to all those who wish to be involved in the city. His prayer should become ours as well:

> Thus I cleanse them from everything foreign, and I establish the duties of the priests and the levites, each in its work; and I provided for the wood offering, at appointed times for the first fruits. Remember me, O my God, for good (Nehemiah 13:30–31).

These four men and these four cities offer a variety of models for the church today in its presence in the urban world. The church in the city is called to a complex task. Though the message and the methods we use are simple, understanding of the complexities around us is required. To those who are called to the proclamation of the gospel, appreciation for the role of the prophet is essential. For those who work diligently and silently behind the scenes in community development, their co-operation with church planters and evangelists is vital. The church of Jesus Christ must develop an integrated approach to the complex urban world in which we live. Doing so will enhance the message of the gospel and increase the impact we have on the lives of men and women.

# CHAPTER 8

# *A Strategy for Reaching Cities*

Though the word 'strategy' seems impersonal and uncaring, it is important for us to ask how a concerned church or individual should approach a city. What strategy or means should be employed in order to make the maximum impact for Christ in seeing people reached with the gospel? The city is so large, contains so many people, has so many needs... where do we start?

There will no doubt be as many approaches to urban mission as there are concerned Christians. This is helpful, particularly if the energy and effort of believers is guided by a biblical vision. The Bible does not hold us to one particular approach to ministry methodology. The Scriptures unfold a variety of approaches and ministries used by God to impact cities.

But there are certain common elements to biblical urban mission which should be understood by every individual, ministry team, family and church hoping to serve Christ effectively in the city. Moreover, there is a unifying framework which all believers in the city are a part of. This chapter will examine four stages of urban mission that make up this framework and some of the basic elements of each stage.

It should be noted that we are not suggesting formulas that guarantee success, however that is defined. But instead, we are saying that all Christians in the city, no matter what their theological perspective, educational achievement or level of maturity, are members of the whole church in the whole city. Awareness of God's purposes for his church in the city increases our appreciation of others—our unity—and our comprehension of God—our faith.

There is a set of attitudes toward ministry and residence in the city that one could call an 'entrance strategy' to urban mission, something that is pre-mission in nature. Some of these attitudes have been touched on already: genuine love for people, faith in God in spite of great need, and giving up our rights.

One more attitude warrants mentioning here, and that is teachableness. If we come to the city as learners, rather than evangelists, social-workers, families-on-a-mission-for-God, churches-that-care, or whatever else we dream up as our reason to be in the city, we will be protected from making a million mistakes and we will be far more Christlike in the process.

Living in the city is a learning process. We will learn about cultures, people, life, pain, ourselves, failure, and if we learn all these lessons, along the way we will learn to be God's answer to others.

We will use the apostle Paul as a model for urban strategy. His life more than any other demonstrates an integrated approach to urban mission and evangelism. (This is not meant to detract from the life of Christ, but in a unique way Paul was commissioned by the Lord Jesus to pioneer the presence of the church in the cities of that day.)

**Conversion of sinners**

In his very helpful book, *Apostles to the City,* Roger Greenway points out that Paul's strategy in cities had a definite pattern:

> The lines of Paul's urban strategy ran from converts, to churches, to the whole Roman society—its governments, institutions and religions. Paul moved out into the highly urbanized Roman world of his day with a definite strategy in mind. (*Apostles to the City,* page 81.)

Paul consciously targeted cities. He focused on the major urban centres of his day. Philippi was a major administrative centre and was situated on an important trade route. Thessalonica was a strategic port for the Roman navy, located on the Ignatian Way. Corinth was provincial capital for Achaia, a port, banking centre and home of the Ismian games. The list goes on: Athens, Rome, Ephesus, Jerusalem.

In these cities Paul believed God for converts. No matter the political, social or spiritual state of affairs, he preached the gospel. His missionary strategy was built on the bedrock of personal conversion. He stood counter to Roman emperor worship and Hellenistic syncretism; to the Jews he declared that Jesus was the Christ, the long-awaited Messiah.

The heart of authentic urban strategy is bringing people to Christ. This is the touchstone of all we do in the city. Whether we are involved with the poor or the rich, the powerless or the powerful, our presence should be motivated by the desire to see people lay down their reasons for rejecting Christ and embrace him as their Lord and Saviour.

We are not speaking of easy-believism. The city does not need a light-weight, superficial gospel that promises everything for nothing. Sinners are rebels. No matter what their class in society, each man and woman has personally ratified Adam's rebellion against God and needs to be confronted with Christ's claim of lordship on their life. The rich man must surrender his wealth and the poor man his bitterness; each person will stand before God to give an account of his life.

## Care for the poor

The agonising question of whether we should preach the gospel or care for the poor is not a biblical one. There is no dichotomy in the Scriptures between caring and preaching. People are created in God's image, body and soul. Therefore, we are to do both.

Evangelists should not proclaim the gospel in situations where there is no expression of commitment to the poor. They have a responsibility to identify with a caring community of believers so that their proclamation is seen to be part of Christ's concern for the felt needs of those they are preaching to.

And the ones caring for the poor must never do so without knowing that their care is done in the name of Christ. Christian organisations cannot accept government offers to serve in a nation without the freedom to do so in Jesus' name.

The apostle Paul demonstrated his concern for the poor, to the point of turning away from his desire to go to Spain and 'fully preach the gospel of Christ, thus making it my ambition to preach the gospel, not where Christ had already been named' (Romans 15:19–20). Instead, Paul persevered in his commitment to those suffering from famine in Jerusalem, in spite of repeated warnings that he would be imprisoned if he returned to that city.

**Church planting among the unreached**

The third stage of urban strategy is church planting. Paul was not satisfied with bringing individuals to Christ. He was concerned with winning sheep *and* building flocks. He gathered believers together wherever he preached, and the organising of churches was central to his entire approach in the city.

Paul was assigned the task of planting churches as an apostle and pioneer of the faith. His zeal in planting churches was based on his revelation of the importance of the body of Christ.

> By revelation he had come to understand that the church was the long-awaited messianic community, the bearer of the gospel to all races and nations. It was through the church that God would now fulfill his redemptive purpose for the world. (*Apostles to the City,* page 8.)

That insight made Paul a church planter. He believed that God in Christ was carrying out his long-awaited redemptive work in the world through the church.

We need the same revelation as Paul. Not only is the church the covenant community of God's people on earth, it is the only way traumatised masses of urban poor will find healing and hope for their broken lives. Through joyful, worshipping, caring communities they have hope. The church is one of God's primary ways of channelling love and hope to his people.

Evangelism for Paul meant not only proclaiming

the gospel, but gathering those who believed into visible, caring communities. Since God's redemptive work in the world was to be carried out through the church, Paul gave the highest priority to establishing organised congregations.

## Commitment to Christ's lordship over the whole of society

Paul planted the seeds in his preaching and teaching that would eventually lead the early church to proclaim Christ's lordship over every aspect of society. His vision of the kingdom touched all dimensions of life. He addressed the role of government (Romans 13), the relationship of slaves to their masters (Philemon; Ephesians 5), the nature and function of the family (Ephesians 5) and the responsibilities of the rich to the poor (1 Timothy 6). There is a refreshing breadth to Paul's teaching that is often missed by the church today. Though he was a church planter and evangelist, his comprehensive view of the lordship of Christ was far more extensive than many realise.

Because he did not challenge the institution of slavery head on, that does not mean he did not address the necessity of its demise. And because he did not write one of his epistles specifically on the subject of injustice, that does not mean Paul was silent on the economic and political issues of his day (eg 1 Timothy 6:2; 2 Thessalonians 3:6–12; Titus 3:1).

Paul not only instilled in his converts a love for the lost, he also taught and encouraged them to take up their responsibilities as contributing members of the cities and nations they inhabited. He also challenged the idols of his day. The riots in Ephesus that resulted from Paul's prophetic preaching let the church know that political and economic issues were the concern of the church.

If churches and missionaries fail to understand that Jesus intends his lordship to be over all of life, they will not be able to disciple the future leaders of the cities they are reaching with the gospel. It is natural for an evangelist to want all his converts to be evangelists as well. But some are called to be bankers, lawyers, educators, government officials and spokesmen in the media.

The churches Paul planted were the leaven of society. They were to be models of righteousness. Paul knew that the men and women he won to Christ were to be formed into congregations, and then sent into the world as salt and light. Some were to be missionaries to the unreached. Others were to be God's agents in the market place or the military. Instructed in God's ways, they became aware of the issues they faced and the great difference between their faith and the idolatries around them. To quote Greenway, 'Gradually the false gods of Rome were identified, the battle joined, and the idols began to fall' (*Apostles to the City*, page 86).

Bible-believing Christians, particularly Christians who are city-dwellers, must perceive the issues of righteousness and justice, know where to draw the battle lines, and engage the demonic urban idols challenging Christ's rulership over every aspect of city life.

## A declaration of war

In every stage of urban mission, believers should be closely related to a local church, ministering in close-knit teams, and acquainted with the power of the Holy Spirit (Romans 15:19a). Urban mission is warfare. To proclaim Christ's kingdom is to challenge

Satan's kingdom. Urban idols are demonic in nature, and when believers appear on the scene we threaten the domination that powers and principalities have had over people's lives.

The presence of the church in the city is a sign to the powers that their hold on people is at an end. The church is a sign of God's redeeming grace. Our presence in a neighbourhood is a living symbol of Christ's power to conquer any bondage. No wonder the demons make such a fuss when the church moves in. But to those who understand the spirits of the city and the urban mission of the church, it is confirmation of Christ's victory.

# PART 4

# FAMILIES IN THE CITY

# CHAPTER 9

## *Parenthood in Peril*

'The family' no longer exists in the Western world. In its place are many families, of diverse styles and shapes. There are single-parent families, step-families, gay families, and non-marital families. We are living through a period of historic change in the structure and function of the family.

The upheaval is evident everywhere in our culture. To quote one magazine, 'Babies have babies ... kids refuse to grow up and leave home, affluent yuppies prize their BMWs more than their children, rich and poor children alike blot their minds with drugs, people casually move in with each other and out again' (*Newsweek* Special Edition, 'The 21st Century Family', Winter/Spring 1990).

Human society is increasingly dominated by urban life, and this has particularly affected the family. The century of industrial development from the 1830s to the 1930s saw a marked increase in the percentage of the British population in urban areas. The percentage rose from approximately 35% to 80%, and now stands at 90%. In the United States 73% of the population is urbanised.

Population centres in Great Britain suffer from economic decline, physical decay and social disintegration and are now commonly referred to as 'Urban Priority Areas'. UPAs, as these places of severe increasing deprivation are called, are characterised by high unemployment, old people living alone, single-parent families, high proportions of ethnic communities, overcrowded homes and a shortage of basic amenities.

The loss of manufacturing jobs from the major cities of Great Britain was particularly dramatic in the 1960s: 50% in Greater London since 1960 and 40% of the other main population centres. The inner cities of today are the industrial centres of the last century. Nineteenth-century industrialisation required rapid-built housing on a large scale to accommodate the labour force. Much of it was substandard.

The report of the Archbishop of Canterbury's commission on the city says,

> The people living in the urban priority areas are not only typically living on a lower income level, and share poor housing standards, but are also exposed to more difficult social relations. Vandalism is rife. Crime rates, or at least reported crimes, have been rising since mid-century, and bear particularly hard on people living in the districts where poverty and deprivation are concentrated. (*Faith in the City*, page 20.)

These factors and many others have contributed to the disintegration of the family in the United Kingdom. While the government's approach has been wilfully inadequate, amounting to little more than first-aid treatment for areas of acute need, the church has responded in the same fashion. In *Faith in the City* not one whole page was devoted to the need of the family in urban priority areas. Many issues such as unemployment, powerlessness, and the role of the church was addressed, but little or nothing was said about the family throughout the entire book. The church's response to the break-up of the family and the pressures it faces in the modern urbanised West is sadly lacking in relevance and urgency.

The divorce rate for families in the United States has doubled since 1965, and sociologists predict that half of all first marriages will end in divorce. Six out of ten second marriages will collapse. One third of all the children born in Western nations will most likely live in a step-family before they are eighteen years of age.

Children are paying the price for their parents' confusion. Two-thirds of all mothers are in the labour force, and more than half of all mothers of infants. Divorce has left a devastated generation in its wake, and for many children the pain is compounded by confusion due to materialistic indulgence, neglect, lack of discipline, and often abject poverty. It is estimated that over 70% of all violent-impulse crimes in Great Britain and the United States are committed by the children of single-parent families.

Western Christians are fearful for the family in the future. They are just beginning to face the reality that exchanging old-fashioned family values for financial independence and a comfortable lifestyle is exacting a very high price. People are beginning to face up to the reality that husbands, wives and children are not getting enough out of family life. People are hurting. The family in Western society has become dysfunctional.

The biblical definition of a family is that a man and woman love each other, are committed to each other through marriage, and raise children in an atmosphere of trust, commitment and loving discipline. By contrast, the American census bureau has settled on another definition of the family: 'two or more persons related by birth, marriage or adoption who reside in the same household'. New York state's highest court stretched this definition recently, and held that the survivor of a gay couple retained the legal right to an apartment they had long shared, just as a surviving husband or wife would.

But to call homosexual households 'families' is ridiculous. One social critic says, 'You can't fool mother nature. The family is a mummy and a daddy and their children.'

Most Christians are yet to take seriously the effects of the industrial revolution on the family. The family was once a close-knit unit of production, held together by the need to support one another. The modern family is now a unit of consumption. The old values of work, savings and family togetherness have been replaced by ideals of financial independence and rapid affluence. The modern family is driven by the twin goals of prosperity and independence. Wealth and comfort are now seen as rights rather than the results of hard work.

The industrial revolution also led to vast changes in *how* we live. The car, television, telephone, jet airplane and the computer have had a profound impact on the modern family. The members of a family that once found their relationships spontaneously by living in a neighbourhood or in a rural setting, now have to choose to have fellowship by getting in their car and driving across town. The family that was once held together by work is now pulled apart by television and the car.

Under the pressures of these developments, the

family has become so fluid that it is hard to identify in Western societies. The heterosexual, nuclear family is fast becoming a vestige of a bygone age. Figures from annual consensus reports reveal that fewer than 27% of the United States' 91 million households in 1988 fit the traditional model of the family. At the same time the census bureau counted 1·6 million same-sex couples living together. In these families there is no longer a mother and a father but a dad and a poppa, or a mum and a mummy. In lesbian 'families', sperm banks have replaced fathers.

**Youthhood**

Sociologist Kenneth Woodward declares, 'The age of extended adolescence has arrived.' Adolescence is a time of intense self-absorption and learning—a time when young people find out who they are and what their philosophy of life is.

Adulthood, on the other hand, is a time to develop character and the other qualities of life that are essential to live as a mature member of society. Such character traits as initiative, competence, commitment, determination, honesty and integrity are all part of this 'growing up' process. By these standards, young people entering the twenty-first century are far less mature than their ancestors. The generation of baby-boomer kids are maturing earlier than previous generations, but emotionally they are taking longer to develop adult attachments. More young people are involved in university and college, but fewer are graduating. They take longer to establish a career and wait longer to get married. They postpone adult choices and spurn long-term commitments.

'Youthhood' is the extended period of life between adolescence and adulthood. Christian leaders mourn the loss of mature teenagers. In generations past youth could be counted on to be emotionally reliable. The present generation is a product of an extremely affluent society and is not willing to pay the price to enter the world of hard realities. Many come from dysfunctional families—some experts estimate that over 60% of British teenagers have experienced sexual or physical abuse.

By the time they reach eighteen years of age 57% of American teenagers have had sex. This is the generation of the one-night stand. More than two-thirds of all abortions are performed on single women under the age of twenty-seven. Unfortunately it is a generation of multiple abortions. The ease with which these young people choose to abort reflects a disturbing sense of self- absorption and an alarming indifference to the moral gravity of their actions.

In fact this is the generation that is committed not to be committed. Half of all thirty-year-olds cohabit before marriage. Many are of the assumption that marriage won't work for the long haul. Studies now demonstrate that couples that cohabit before marriage are more likely to divorce than those who do not.

The influence of television, with its ability to provide instant, incessant and intellectually passive diversion, is a major cause of protracted immaturity. The endless hours of watching the tube and listening to pop music has bred a passive population of young people.

The evidence of this passivity can be found in the changing vision that students have of life after college. One sociologist points out that in the early 70s the most cherished value of life for university students was developing a meaningful philosophy of life. But by the end of the 80s that value had dropped to ninth, far behind the first choice of 'being well-off financially'.

## International trends

Unfortunately, these trends are not limited to the American or British scene. Nearly half of all children born in Denmark, Iceland and Sweden are born out of wedlock. Shunning the word 'illegitimate', demographers now refer to children born out of wedlock as 'non-marital children'.

Four out of seven marriages in Sweden fail—one of the highest divorce rates in the Western world. In the 20 to 30 age group half of Sweden's couples who live together are unmarried.

Legislators in Sweden have granted unmarried partners living together an equal legal status with married couples. Tax questions, rental agreements, insurance issues and other judicial matters increasingly lead to calls to confer equal status, whether it involves heterosexual or homosexual partners. According to *World Christian News,* Denmark became the first country to legalise homosexual unions in October 1989. Although the 'registered partnerships' are not called marriages, their legal ramifications approximate to heterosexual matrimony.

## The Blacks and the boomers

Two extremes of family life in America and Britain flow side by side and yet never seem to touch one another. The one common denominator is the break-up of the family. Both the baby-boomer generation, those born between 1946 and 1964, and urban Blacks are affected by family break-up.

The baby boomers were brought up in the most

affluent society in human history, yet they display an undercurrent of dissatisfaction, a feeling that something has gone very wrong with their world. The boomers have become the yuppies, and they have learned that even two-income families cannot buy happiness.

On the other side of the city—economically and physically—live urban Blacks. Harvie Conn, Editor of *Urban Mission*, says,

> Of all Americans, they appear to be most vulnerable to current trends of family disillusion. As long ago as 1982 almost 30% of all black families were female-headed households with children, in contrast to 7% of white families.

Break-up of the Black family lends itself to racist stereotypes. Many Whites assume that Blacks are 'immoral, irresponsible, and incapable of keeping their families together'.

Some people call this the syndrome of 'blaming the victim'. The sickness of the Black family is assumed to be the cause of the deterioration of the Black community, rather than the symptom. This kind of superficial thinking goes no further than the end of our nose.

However, Black pastor Wellington Boone asserts that it is the welfare system that led to the break-up of the Black family. 'Slavery decimated the Black family. After the Civil War Blacks began to rebuild the traditional family values brought with them from Africa. Then liberals with their vision of a great society began to hand out money to solve problems that they were not willing to get involved with on a personal basis.' Boone and many other Blacks believe that the welfare system contributed to the break-up of the family, encouraging Black fathers not to marry so that the per-child-diem would continue.

At the same time, urban Black families have learned to develop resources to draw on that most Whites have never dreamed about. Neighbours develop a close community to help provide support in raising children. The Black extended family reaches past blood lines and turns next-door neighbours into 'uncles' and 'aunts'. Further, Black men have developed a 'soul brother' relationship.

By the year 2000, there will be 40 million Hispanics in the United States. White Christians have much to learn from traditional Hispanic family life. The strong bonds of family commitment in the Hispanic culture are a model to study closely. Though the strength of the family is now being challenged by gangs and drugs, much can be learned from them about what the post-suburban Western world should look like. This is in spite of the fact that economic pressures have forced many Hispanic men to leave their families in Mexico and Central America. At present one third of all Hispanic children live in single-parent homes in the United States.

## Families in need

That the family is in trouble is a fact questioned by no one. Of the 33 million poor Americans whose incomes fall below the poverty line, 13 million are children. 500,000 of those are homeless. Two million American children have been dropped from school lunch programmes since 1980. Thirty per cent of US high-school students don't graduate. For non-Whites the drop-out rate is over 40%.

Christians have answers for these problems. The most basic unit in society, even more basic than the church, is the family. In the opening pages of the Bible God describes his intent for a man and woman to cleave together and raise children in an atmosphere of godly love and purity. The salvation of the family in Great Britain lies not only in the proclamation of the gospel, but in Christian families themselves finding new meaning and purpose by a commitment to Christian service. In order for the Christian family to find focus it must be a family that commits itself to sacrificial service to others. The opportunities are there for those who want to get involved.

# CHAPTER 10

## *Families with a Mission*

To the Editor
*Christianity Today*
Wheaton, Illinois,
USA

Dear Sir,

I apologize for the lateness of my letter. I just read an article in *Christianity Today* entitled, 'Growing up a World Away' (February 89). I felt that there was something I really wanted to share about this article.

I am an MK [missionaries' kid]. My parents were missionaries in a central Asian country where I was born, and I now live in the Netherlands where I have grown up. I found your article fascinating but there was something I found was missing.

My parents have always *included* us in our choices on 'the missionfield'. They have encouraged us to pray and ask God for His guidance, personally, for all the decisions we make.

I would like to suggest when God calls 'Mom and Dad' to be missionaries He is not forgetting their children! I have asked for, and received, a very personal calling and burden for the country we live in. God has called me too! And if God has called me, no blame can rest on my parents. We were encouraged to pray about what kind of schooling we should have and as a result my brother and I have chosen two different schools (he attended an international school, I attended a Dutch public school). So any adjustment I might have to make, or extra schooling I'll have to do, if I feel God is wanting me to attend college in the States, is just that—an adjustment I'll have to make. It is not a major problem. I believe it might even be part of God's over-all plan for my life.

Problems/questions should not be missionaries' children and their schooling—the question should be: have I asked God what He wants? And I really missed hearing that in your article. God created the family and He doesn't just call half of it, He calls it as a whole. Kids need to be encouraged to grasp and accept that calling for themselves personally. Any resentment a kid might feel is probably because he is dragged along and not included in those decisions that so majorly affect his life, too! God knows what is best for us.

Why not ask Him?! (And ask Him *with* your children!)

Sincerely
Misha McClung (16)

## Growing up in a city

Growing up in a city, just like growing up on the missionfield, has a certain amount of glory and a certain amount of pain. Misha's letter reflects some of the glory.

When you raise kids biculturally and bilingually, include them in the decisions that affect their lives, they grow up with an excitement about hearing God's voice for themselves.

Raising kids in a city, just like in a missionfield, has

its disadvantages. Sometimes they are not able to play outside with the other kids; it is too rough or dangerous. Often there is no place to play. But the glory of living in the city far outweighs the pain. In fact the pain becomes glorious when we look at it in the right way. The glory of God is often found in the most difficult circumstances. Who would have thought that God would have sent *his* Son to suffer the humiliating, cruel and painful death of the cross? But in that horrendous moment, the magnificence of God's goodness and glory is fully manifested.

The glory of raising kids in the city has to do with the magnificence of God's Spirit fleshed out in our lives in the neighbourhoods, council estates and suburbs where we live. The glory of God is the triumph of his grace meeting people's needs in real-life situations. The glory is seeing our children get involved in other people's lives and learn to rely on God's Spirit in those situations.

In the early years of our ministry, I saw too much glory in my 'ministry' and it caused me to spend too much time away from home. I actually missed the glory of our home as I immersed myself in hours of counselling and street evangelism and responding to the physical needs of people around us. Fortunately, my dear wife Sally would not let me escape into my own little world of glory; the faithful reminder of her needs and those of our two children rescued me from my own inglorious fate.

Today, having lived in the city of Amsterdam since 1971, the glory far outshines the pain. Our kids have grown, and have turned out beautifully. This city has definitely helped shape them into the vibrant, concerned, thoughtful, international kids they are. To quote one Christian leader, 'If we could do it all over again, we would do it all over again.'

Through the years of living in Christian community, having raised two very honest children and having a very practical wife, we have learned lessons about what we would do differently if there were a next time. The question of families raising kids in the city is a complex and multifaceted one, and as I said, full of both pain and glory. No family situation is the same as another. No two cities are the same, no two suburbs are the same, no two families are the same, and no two perceptions are the same.

**The pain**

It is important to face honestly the disadvantages of raising kids in the city.

*The pain of mistrust.* There is the pain of racial separation in the city. White kids are often a minority and they feel like it. This separation affects the playtime of children. They cannot talk to strangers, they cannot play in the park, they cannot go outside after dark, they never open the door when their parents are gone, they don't leave their bicycle outside (or it's gone), and they have to be very careful to pay attention to what is going on around them.

White parents who live in Asian, Black or Hispanic neighbourhoods must also face the pain of separation. There may be mistrust. Ethnic minorities look with suspicion upon Whites who move into their neighbourhood. White do-gooders are not wanted, although genuine friends are.

*The pain of time limits.* For parents who live in challenging neighbourhoods there is the constant opportunity to care not only for their own children but for the children of others as well. Because they are surrounded by families and children in need there is a tremendous pull on their time to be involved with lots of house guests. Busy mums and dads are also pulled into church gatherings, community meetings and responses to late-night emergencies.

*The pain of physical danger.* Walking down the street and being confronted with a knife or getting knocked off your bicycle is not a lot of fun. Being a woman and always fearing a physical attack is not an easy pressure to live with.

*The pain of sensory overload.* Children and parents learn to live with continual input to the eyes, ears and noses. There are rancid smells from walls on which people have urinated. The sound of traffic and street conversation is ever present. Some cultures find this sensory input a painful process, but for others it is the very essence of life. The busyness, the close contact, the sights and the sounds of the city create a sense of security and well-being for many cultures.

## The glory

When God's character is fleshed out in real-life family situations, the consequence is principles learned. Those principles work in every culture. Before we look at the principles and how to apply them, let us first look at some of the reasons why urban life can be so glorious. The following are quotes taken from my son Matthew about why he enjoyed urban life:

- ▷ Something that I like about the city is that it doesn't lack in excitement—there is always something to do and it's not real boring.
- ▷ In this city in particular, transportation is good; you don't always have to rely on cars to take you around.
- ▷ This city has a nice atmosphere to it. I know there are some thieves and criminals and so on, but the majority

of the population are not like that and there is just a sense of a lot of people being together in one place. That's nice.

▷ The city is like a two-faced place. There are nice people and there are unkind people. You have to watch your back now and then so that you don't get robbed or mugged or anything, but you can meet people here, you can have friendships.

▷ There is no lack of activity. There are plenty of things to do, such as playing billiards or going swimming, going for a walk in the park, going to a movie, going out for dinner. There are lots of different types of restaurants here from all different countries in the world. Shopping is also very convenient to do.

Another aspect that Matthew finds fascinating about this city has to do with the international dimension:

▷ There are lots of different cultures here. You can meet lots of really interesting people—people from all over the world, such as people from Africa, South America, the Caribbean, Asia.

Matthew also made a comment about growing up in two cultures.

▷ The education here in Amsterdam is quite a bit better than in the States, and you get a much more wide view. In the States your view tends to be quite narrow, but here you have many different experiences.

City life is also fascinating because of the kinds of urban activities that you don't find in a small town:

▷ There are lots of different parades. We see the Dutch Santa Claus come in every year. There are lots of protests, demonstrations, all sorts of different things that we get to see here that you don't have in little tiny St Nowhere in Iowa.

## No pain—no gain

As a parent I have tried conscientiously to reflect over the benefits versus the disadvantages for my children in raising them in the city. One wonderful benefit is cross-cultural sensitivity. Children learn what it is like to be discriminated against. They also learn to see people as real people and not as stereotypes or caricatures. They see and taste foods from all over the world. They experience people struggling with pressures and opportunities that in their own culture they would never experience. They see lonely children on the streets. The effects of alcohol, drugs and promiscuous sex is ever present before their eyes. Shelter them from this? No way. I hope it affects them to the point they do not want to get involved. I pray God will use it to shape their values and ambition in life.

Another benefit of urban life comes when children learn that everything in life is a gift from God and that those of us who have a secure home and an intact family are immensely blessed. Our children have learned to live in two worlds, the world of their home culture and the world of their adopted culture. They learn that they are indeed pilgrims on this earth.

Not only do our children have the opportunity to learn this but we as parents do as well. It was quite difficult for me when we took our children back to the States and they did not know the pledge of allegiance to the flag, something every American school child learns.

Sally was shocked when she tried to explain to Matthew how important the Alamo is in the history of Texas, her home state. To her attempts at a spontaneous history lesson about the great Republic of Texas, Matthew quipped, 'Isn't the Alamo a rent-a-car agency?' Sally's face revealed her disappointment that her son did not share the deep feelings she had as a Texan embodied in the words 'Remember the Alamo'.

Urban children are raised in a spiritual environment that is forged out of necessity. To be living as strangers in a neighbourhood among people from different nationalities is a tremendous challenge to the prayer life and the commitment of a family. Children can have a vision instilled into them for ministry and for the world that will never come by living in cultural and ethnic insularity.

Children learn about the fallen nature of man in a city. The city contains both the best and the worst of human nature and human civilisation. Crime *is* in the city. Children see before them the fallen nature of man and have the opportunity to respond on a daily basis.

To quote the son of one urban pastor,

> Children learn that by moving to the city they are not going to be there primarily to help fend for the poor and the sick and the needy; what they are more likely to learn is that their character is going to be developed and their soul will be deeply impacted by being incarnated in real humanity. The lessons that their souls learn from their physical environment cannot be equated in the American success formula.

Children do not learn much when their only experience of the city is to 'roll up your windows and lock your doors!' Children raised in fear become self-centered and paranoid. Instead of learning that the church is truly international and made up of people of all colors and nations, they learn to keep their distance from those who are different. Children are not stupid; they learn whom they ought to fear and whom they can trust by watching their parents. They learn who are the 'good' guys and who are the 'bad' guys.

Urban living is no antidote to raising fearful and self-centered children. Within the inner city they too can learn to exclude and to fear. However, exclusion in the city cannot go unnoticed. The great shame of the suburbs is that they do not even know who they are or what they are doing. Within the city, racism and conspicuous consumption are obvious. Perhaps that is the key to some of our problems. Certain environments allow lies to continue, while others force us to face them. (Paul Van der Klay, *Urban Mission*, Volume 7, No. 2.)

## Principles for raising children in the city

You decide to commit yourselves, as a family, to the city—what now? Here are some often very practical points to bear in mind.

*God calls the whole family*. If we include our children in the process of seeking God for his will for the family, it gives us the opportunity to teach them to hear God's voice. They can know for themselves that the Lord is calling them into Christian service by being a part of a family in mission. Children learn from their parents, and it has been our approach from our children's earliest days that they were to be a part of our ministry. God has a role for them to play.

I was thrilled when my twelve-year-old daughter came home from a camp, and said to me: 'Uncle Dale said that I have a destiny. He said every child in every family has a destiny. What is my destiny, Daddy?' I was excited because Misha heard what I deeply believed and had tried to model to her all of her life. God has a destiny for every child and for every family. The process of creating a sense of adventure and faith in the heart of a child is easy for children to learn. When they see us expectantly asking our Father for his direction and confirmation for how our family can be a blessing to others, the enthusiasm catches.

*A second important principle in raising children in the city is teaching them that they have a specific role to play in ministering to people.* We taught our children how important it was to love the prostitutes and to treat them as normal human beings. We encouraged them to be friendly, to wave and also to draw pictures for them at school. Of course this gave us the opportunity to teach our children about the dangers of paternalism, and how to respond to people when we do not agree with their lifestyle.

This whole process paid off wonderfully, when after a long time one of our children gave a picture to a particular prostitute named Betty. One day she could not resist the temptation and came to our little home in the middle of the red light district to drink coffee and ask questions about who we were. It wasn't too much later that she accepted Christ as her Saviour. And it was through this experience that Misha and Matthew began to learn that God could use them as well as their Mum and Dad.

*We help our children grow in discernment and maturity by dealing with the spirits of the city.* We teach them the difference between cultural patterns and spiritual powers. It is very important from an early age to teach our children how Satan attacks people in their minds, their bodies and in their emotions.

We must teach them how to respond to such things as violence, hurriedness, impersonalness, sexual immorality, racism, economic injustice, materialism, greed and anger. These spiritual forces are at work in the city and in the hearts of the people of the city. We do this by evaluating each situation as it comes up and teaching them God's response in that situation.

*We should teach our children practical lessons of 'urban survival'.* This includes how to get around in the city on public transport, how to respond to strangers, where they can go and when they can't go and how they should walk when they are there. Kids are not stupid. They learn from their parents—what they see more than what they hear. If we are fearful of the city they will pick up our attitudes immediately, but if on the other hand we look to the Lord for his protection and his wisdom in every situation, they will develop that as an attitude of life. We must take the initiative with our children and look for those 'teachable moments'.

*We serve our children by teaching them about modesty and purity.* We allowed the questions our kids asked to set the agenda of what we taught them. What we explained to Matthew as a five-year-old when he asked what the prostitutes did, and what we said when he was eight years old, and then twelve years old, were all quite different.

Misha answered the question the first time! When they were five and seven years old we took them into the city to visit. We were trying to introduce them to the city in a positive way, doing fun things with them and helping them adjust to inner-city living. One night we were looking for a parking place and ended up in the red-light district trying to get to the place we were staying. Matthew saw all the ladies standing in the windows with hardly any clothes on and exclaimed from the back seat, 'Look Mummy, what are all those ladies doing without any clothes on?' Immediately Misha piped up and said, 'Well Matthew, when you do things you shouldn't do, after a while you begin to think that they are the right things to do. These ladies are breaking God's laws and now they think it is OK to break God's laws. If we do what is wrong then we'll start believing it is right.'

Sally was both amazed and amused at Misha's answer. Amazed at her maturity and amused at how she was teaching her little brother. Later she discussed it in more depth with Matthew and Misha and explained exactly God's point of view towards people who break his laws. That night the lesson had to do with breaking God's laws, not so much with what the ladies were doing. She simply explained that they were immodest and that they did things that broke God's heart. She also explained how important it was to love them and pray for them.

*We help our children by realising that life takes more time in the city.* The pressures of busy urban life mean kids are going to need more time for sleep. They are going to need more time with their parents. This means parents must slow down. It just simply takes more time to handle all the situations and pressures that arise. It has to be worked into our schedule whether we are involved in 'Christian ministry' or whether we made a commitment to a neighbourhood because God has called us to be there.

*Another practical principle is that we have to adjust child-care equipment and toys.* You have to have strollers (push-chairs) that fit on buses, rain gear that can fit in your bag and toys that can be used primarily inside the house.

Sally learned during the early days of raising our

kids in the city how important it was for her to make the home a place of warmth and refreshment, a place of creativity and acceptance. Parents set the mood by their attitudes, their words and the choices they make.

*It is important to provide places and opportunities for our children to be involved in sports clubs and other activities that give them proper physical exercise.* Some inner-city playgrounds are adequate. There are also swimming pools, football clubs, bicycle paths, basketball courts, etc, that may be available.

Sometimes the play must be supervised. There is no reason why parents should not organise the needed oversight. Talk with other concerned parents and get involved in activities with your children. Not only does this give an opportunity for them to grow properly physically, but it also keeps parents involved with their children.

*Another principle is to teach our children to trust God by giving them special faith projects.* To illustrate how we did this when we moved into one inner-city apartment, we challenged our children (who were seven and nine at the time) to take on the challenge to pray in the finances to furnish their bedrooms. Our kids got very excited and involved in this project. They baked cookies and sold them, collected old things and sold them door to door, and shared the need with their friends.

Cheques came from grandparents, people bought things, friends gave unexpected gifts and slowly their bank accounts mounted up. Their sense of accomplishment and trust in the Lord grew tremendously as they saw the money come in to help purchase furniture for their own rooms. They were a part of what was happening. It was a great experience for all of us.

*It is important to help our children enjoy the city.* Too often we are 'in the city but not of it'. Don't keep the city at a distance. Celebrate its life: go to the theatre, the concerts, the parks, the zoos, the museums; walk its streets and meet its people. Love the city and your kids will love it too.

*It is important to have regular family times.* When our kids were infants, although Sally and I were not breakfast-eaters, we decided to make breakfast time a very important family event. We both got up, helped get the kids dressed and spent time together over the breakfast table. That tradition carried on until they were teenagers.

We prayed over the day and committed our lives to the Lord. At night I would help get the children ready for bed while Sally prepared meals. After the meal, I would tell them stories. I made up stories about Peter the Church Mouse, Wally the Whale and Billy Bass the evangelist.

As the children got older we began to read good books with them. We went through *The Little House on the Prairie* series, C.S. Lewis's *Narnia Chronicles*, J.R.R. Tolkien's *The Lord of the Rings*, Kenneth Grahame's *The Wind in the Willows* and many others. What a wonderful experience this was together as a family. It gave us many opportunities to share and talk about how things were going in their lives—and they developed a love for good literature as well.

As the kids got older, our family times changed to become a weekly event. Eventually, we called the family meetings as we needed them. They are still a regular part of our family life. Family meetings became a time for fun, for prayer, for personal sharing, for decision-making and for conflict resolution. It created a sense of family cohesiveness and togetherness.

*Another principle is that of looking for God's compensations in the midst of sacrifice.* There is no denying the fact that you give up something to live in some parts of the city. However, I learned something very important from Sally. Early on she developed an attitude of looking for God's compensations. If she gave up something in one part of her life that was important to her, she believed the Lord would make it up in another way. I am not talking about material things. Often it would just be that the Lord would send along a friend to spend time with her, or that somebody would write a letter, or that we would do something special as a family.

The most important part of this attitude was the fact that Sally went through life looking for God's goodness in the little and big things of life. She has passed this attitude on to me and to our children, and it has been a wonderful blessing to us all.

*There is no substitute for listening to our children.* I realised early on in my life that we needed to do things together that would allow me to hear the heart of my kids. I believed strongly that if my kids were to enter into my world, I first needed to enter their world. I believed I was to create a bridge through friendship that would allow them to know they could talk to me or to Sally any time they wanted.

Matthew and I often played snooker together. We also developed a passion for video games. Misha and I have often gone to movies, to a museum, or out for a drink of hot chocolate. Sally does the same thing with the kids regularly, having special times with each one of them.

These are times to listen to our children. Often the parents speak and the children listen. But we need to learn to reverse this role and become active listeners. This shows that we consider our children important and that we respect their feelings and emotions.

We have always encouraged our kids to share honestly with us their feelings, taking them seriously and letting them know that whatever they feel, we accept them. I believe it is important to show them by our attitude they can be honest with us and with God.

*We tried to teach our children dependence upon the Lord by praying about everything that happens in our lives.* I believe it is extremely important to give our kids an opportunity to share their emotions honestly, but then we must go beyond that to telling God how we feel. By praying together with our children and encouraging them to express their hearts to God, we teach them that God is trustworthy, that he is accepting, that he is patient and that he has time for them.

And when the answers come to their prayers, they learn that God is involved in their lives. Obviously we have to teach them that he answers in ways we do not expect or that we do not like as well.

*Another principle is to teach our children the blessings of hospitality.* Whether we foster children and take them into our homes, invite strangers in for a meal or spend time with our friends, hospitality shows where our priorities are. People are to take precedence over projects and programmes.

We should include our kids in family hospitality. They can participate in the process of preparing as well as cleaning up after meals. Sharing around the meal table with guests and enjoying the people God brings into our home is a great opportunity to learn. What a wonderful privilege we have of letting them get to know men and women of God as well as neighbours, friends and people in need.

Several years ago a really wonderful woman of God singled out our son Matthew after a meal together in our home, and spent hours with him. She shared experiences from her life, and then listened to him for hours as he told about things he enjoyed doing. It was an unexpected fruit of the hospitality of our home and it meant a lot to us and to Matthew.

Some years ago our friends Jim and Rona Gilchrist moved into Otara, a part of Auckland, New Zealand. Auckland is actually the largest Polynesian city in the world. More island people live in Auckland than in any other one city, including the island nations of the South Pacific. When Jim and Rona moved to Otara they had three children.

They were surrounded by gangs of Tongans, Samoans and other island youth. The night they moved into the neighbourhood there was a gang fight on the street in front of them. One gang tried to burn down a house of another gang. Two nights later there was an attempted rape two doors down from them. Right after that there was a murder four doors away.

Jim and Rona felt the Lord had called them to that neighbourhood to be involved in the lives of these young men and women. Over the years they have taken in almost 100 people who have lived in their home. Every single one of them have come and taken up residence, as many as twenty-five at a time.

Has this affected their own three children? Yes, but not negatively. They all love the Lord all the more for Jim and Rona's commitment to get involved with the young people in their city and neighbourhood.

Your family may not be called to live in the red-light district like ours, or to take gang kids in like Jim and Rona Gilchrist, but every family is called. Where your family is called is for you to discover, but called it is.

By committing ourselves to a lifestyle of service in

the city to which God leads us, we not only bring great joy to the heart of our Father in heaven, we also embark on a journey of pain and glory, one that will challenge us, and more important, change us.

It is never too late to start that journey.

# *Bibliography*

*The Urban Christian,* Ray Bakke, MARC, Eastbourne, England.
*Urban Harvest,* Roy Joslin, Evangelical Press, Welwyn, England.
*Cities in New Testament Times,* Charles Ludwig, Accent Books, Denver, Colorado, USA.
*Toward Creative Urban Strategy,* George Torney, Word, Waco, Texas, USA.
*Apostles to the City,* Roger Greenway, Baker, Grand Rapids, Michigan, USA.
*Taking Our Cities for God,* John Dawson, Creation House, Lake Mary, Florida, USA.
*Nine Worlds to Win,* Floyd McClung and Kalafi Moala, Word, England.
*Calling Our Cities to Christ,* Presbyterian and Reformed Publishing Co., Nutley, New Jersey, USA.
*Guidelines for Urban Church Planting,* Roger Greenway, Baker, Grand Rapids, Michigan, USA.
*A Clarified Vision for Urban Mission,* Harvie Conn, Zondervan, Grand Rapids, Michigan, USA.

*The Urban Challenge,* Rose Hadaway, Broadman Press, Nashville, Tennessee, USA.
*The Meaning of the City,* Jacques Ellul.
*World-Class Cities and World Evangelization,* David Barrett, New Hope, Birmingham, Alabama, USA.
*Christ and the Powers,* Hendrik Berkof, Harold Press.
*Faith in the City,* The Report of the Archbishop of Canterbury's Commission on Urban Priority Areas, Church House Publishing, London, England.
*Christianity with Power,* Charles Craft, Vine Books, Ann Arbor, Michigan, USA.

# The Father Heart of God

## by Floyd McClung

*What is God like?*

*Has he got time for twentieth-century men and women?*

*Does he really care?*

In his work with *Youth with a Mission*, Floyd McClung has met many who suffer from deep emotional hurts and fears.

Time and again it has been the discovery of God as Father—perfect and reliable, unlike any human parent—that has brought healing and liberty.

This book is for you...

...if you find it hard to accept God as a loving father,
or
...if you know God's love but would like to share his blessing with others more effectively.

# Father, Make Us One

**by Floyd McClung**

Shortly before he died Jesus prayed for Christians today:
'May they be brought to complete unity to let the world know that you sent me . . .'

Christians do not believe all the same things. We do not see eye to eye on all matters. We find some people difficult to understand, difficult to *love*.

So can there be unity?

Floyd McClung offers his answer to that question. He knows the score—it isn't easy. We need to be realistic. Whether it's between individual believers or between whole churches, there is no easy way to unity.

But Christ prayed for it, so it has to be our priority. Unity of the Spirit now—unity of the faith to come. Self-denying love now—triumph over every hurt and misunderstanding a promise for the future.

How much do we want what Jesus wants?

# Where Will I Find the Time?

**by Sally McClung**

*'If I could just get myself organized . . .'*

*'I've got so much to do, I don't know where to begin . . .'*

*'I've found a system to work by, but I don't seem to have time for people any more . . .'*

For most of us, the busier our lives become, the less fulfilled they seem to be. Sally McClung offers realistic advice for all those who want to learn to use time more effectively—for God, for family, for friends. Time to work and play. Most of all, time to live life in such a way that God can use us as he wants.

**Sally McClung** is married to Floyd and has two teenage children. Her active ministry within Youth With A Mission in Amsterdam is carried out within the context of a busy family life. Consequently Sally has learned to budget her time while still remaining flexible and open to the needs of those around her.

# Knowing God's Will

## by Paul Miller

Christians believe that God has revealed his will to men and women down the ages. The Bible is prized as a perfect and fully sufficient record of his dealings with mankind, containing everything we need to know about his will for us in general.

But how do I check out with God my own personal decisions? Is 'sanctified common sense' enough?

What place should I give to the advice of others, and to 'words from the Lord' given in good faith?

How do I know it is God's voice I am hearing, especially when things don't turn out the way I thought he meant them to?

'This is a book that will answer these questions, and many more! I highly recommend it to you.'

—Floyd McClung, Executive Director,
International Operations, Youth With A Mission

**Paul Miller** is the Director of Youth With A Mission in London.

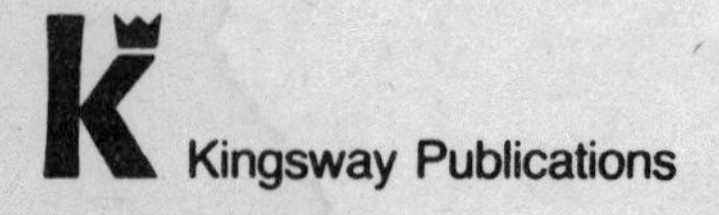

# The Reluctant Evangelist

## by Paul Miller

Of course, not everyone has the gift of evangelism. But has God fallen short in providing too few evangelists?

Paul Miller reminds us that, although God makes great use of lion-hearted souls eager for action, he specialises in the faltering, reluctant hero. People like Moses and Gideon.

People like you?

**PAUL MILLER** has himself come the way of the reluctant evangelist. His work with Youth With A Mission has taken him to Afghanistan, Holland and then England, where he is a member of the senior leadership team. This is his second book, and like *Knowing God's Will* shares lessons learned from both Scripture and often-painful experience.